White Sheets To Brown Babies

White Sheets To Brown Babies

Jvonne Hubbard

ISBN: 0692056866
ISBN 13: 9780692056868

This book is dedicated to Jim. Three really is my lucky number! I love you; this book would not be possible without you. Namaste.

Table of Contents

Preface

WHEN I WAS JUST A little girl no more than six years old, we lived a stone's throw from a Baptist church. When I was five I had attended a vacation Bible school there. Now, a year later, I was inside playing when I heard a child's scream through my parent's open bedroom window. I ran outside to see what had happened. My mom stopped me at the back door though, where she was rushing in. She told me what had happened and what the scream was all about.

Apparently, a group of children who were attending that year's vacation Bible school had begun happily playing on the church's grassy front lawn. My dad had noticed one little black boy amongst the white children, and had hidden himself in the wooded area of our property line to take aim at his little head with a BB gun and shoot him multiple times. A few minutes later my dad came in laughing at how the little "nigger" had run away screaming, probably thinking he was bee-stung. He was proud of the way it had pained the child enough to run him back into the sanctuary of the church.

When things like that make up the totality of your childhood—the most formative years of your life—you don't get away unscathed. In fact, you don't usually get away at all, but I did. Not before much heartache, trauma and sorrow though. That is primarily what this book is about. The things I saw, the things I lived through, the things I survived, the things I experienced and what I became in spite of it all.

Through this book I tell my truth, the whole truth and nothing but the truth, so help me God. For the truth shall set you free. I am not ashamed of the truth, for to be ashamed is to be held prisoner by it. In that vein, I find this life has left me a little rough around the edges. I find I curse to make my point sometimes. My humor can even be a little dark, but it's still my saving grace. I have no secrets. Secrets make you sick. With that said, not everybody feels that way and so some of the people's names in my true story have been changed, either because they requested me to do so and I chose to respect their privacy, or because they were such miserable fucks they didn't deserve to see their name in print! I don't know if love is stronger than hate, but I have found hate to be exhausting.

Daddy's Little Girl

Daddy's little girl, no frilly bows or dresses
Daddy's little girl, no time for frilly messes
Take it like a man, in order to remain
Standing through the fire, standing through the pain
Daddy's little girl, running hard to catch his hand
Daddy's little girl, always looking for the man
The one he never was, the one he should've been
Strong, yet sweetly gentle, the greatest of all men
Daddy's little girl, spits out the grit and dust
Daddy's little girl, watches him go, because he must
He was detached and lonely, unable to commit
Cursed the world for every failure, and never gave a shit
Daddy's little girl, afraid to cry real tears
Daddy's little girl, afraid to feel her fears
The image now lies broken, a heap of history
Daddy's little girl, will always be a part of me

CHAPTER 1

White Sheets

I REMEMBER THE FIRST TIME I became aware of "God" person-ally. I was four and a half years old, standing on a four-foot dirt mound that was piled up where my parents were cutting a drive-way to our home in Brevard, North Carolina.

My grandparents had given my dad a piece of land on one side of their home, and another piece on the other side to my uncle. It was a beautiful spring day and it had started to sprinkle rain. My grandmother Hubbard was sitting on her front porch, her house right beside ours, and as the thunder rolled in the dis-tance I spread my arms wide, lifted my face upwards to the sky, closed my eyes and let the rain come. I was aware of God in that moment, though no one had ever talked about Him the way I was feeling Him.

Then my grandmother yelled from her porch, in the manner with which she usually spoke of God, "You better get in the house little girl, before God strikes you dead with a bolt of lightning!" Without hesitation I responded, "God wouldn't do that to me, He loves me!" And the rain came harder, and the thunder rolled, and

I was sure that I was right. Grandma went in, but I waited until I was soaking wet, then I climbed off the mound unscathed.

However, the world is full of people, life is sometimes cruel, and very few of us remain unscathed whether there is a God to love us, or not. I came into this world as we all do, without prejudice, without hate, without preconceived notions, but the world gets smaller as we grow up and our personal experiences begin to shape and mold us, conform us and change us. For a time, as children we are at the mercy of two main people, for the most part our mother and father. Those two people bear the responsibility of guiding us along this journey; they show us about life by how they live theirs. They teach us by example and set standards of behavior that we emulate in order to develop. But . . . what if they don't? Or worse, what if they do, but they are wrong?

At age five I started kindergarten. Until that point I had been the apple of my mother's eye. She had been a stay-at-home mom until I was four years old, and my dad had worked as a driver for the county's "old folks" center. On weekends we would go camping and fishing as a family. Living beside my paternal grandparents was great because I had a beautiful relationship with my grandpa. I helped him in the garden, and we took daily walks through the expanse of woods behind our homes, me bounding ahead to hide behind every tree, he pretending to be surprised every time I jumped out. Life was beautiful!

When I entered public school at age five, my mom went to work for the county as a janitor. Shortly thereafter my dad stopped working altogether. He began drinking and hosting weekend parties at the house instead of the family camping trips. At first nothing too radical happened. I had cousins my age to play with who came to the parties with their parents. I didn't really care what the adults were up to until strange and scary things started to happen.

The menfolk started putting on weird robes with hoods that covered their faces except for the eye holes. They looked like ghosts to me. Then a strange man in a red robe came to our home and "initiated" all the white-robed men into his club, and gave my dad a green robe and called him the Grand Dragon. They took oaths, performed strange rituals that included flying a flag that didn't look anything like what we pledged allegiance to at school. They brandished weapons and lit crosses instead of campfires. Then everyone would drink alcohol excessively and play unbearably loud country music into the wee hours of the morning.

Sometimes I would hide on top of the washing machine in the hallway and jump out at drunks as they wobbled down the hallway to the bathroom. Often it would cause them to fall out the open back door! For adults, I thought they were acting pretty stupid. I didn't really understand what was going on. My mom told me my dad had joined a club known as the Ku Klux Klan, which sounded funny to me, like the noise our chickens made while clucking around the yard, but I would soon find out there was nothing funny about it.

My grandparents didn't find it funny either, when the loud music and partying kept them awake, or forced them to call the police on their own son. It never seemed to matter, because once the cops were gone, the music would go back up and the drinking would continue. On Sunday mornings after the wild parties were over, I would wake up before any of the passed-out adults and step over sleeping drunks on the floor en route to the kitchen to pour myself some cereal. I would chew my Loops thinking about how stupid these adults were, while considering things like how at their drunkest I would bet them a dollar that I could do magic. Always taking the bait, they would watch me play a game with a set of six coasters turned over where I would predict the color of each one before turning it over to reveal I was right, *every time*. Little did they know that I had identified special nicks and markings on the backside of each one until I had the coaster colors memorized. *Tee hee*, I would think, then go outside and play until the grown-ups woke up.

During the week at school my best friend in the whole world was a little black girl named Yonnie. We sat together, played together, chose each other as partners in games and for every field trip. We were inseparable on the playground, and at lunchtime. We loved each other so much! My mother usually picked me up after school, but one day when I came out it was my dad waiting for me as I climbed into the passenger seat. I could tell he was angry about something and he had an open beer can between his legs. His first words to me as I got in the car were, "Who's the little nigger?"

My dad was near six-foot-three and solidly built, which made for a very intimidating and threatening physical presence, especially when drunk! I did not understand the word nigger, but I could tell he was angry. I answered him with a question. "What do you mean?" He hit the steering wheel hard with his fist and got angrier. "I saw you out there," he said, as he gestured towards the playground, "romping around and wallowing with that little nigger!" Puzzled and growing increasingly scared I replied with another question. "Yonnie?"

"Oh, is that the little nigger's name?" he sneered. By now I was crying. I didn't understand why my daddy was so angry with me for playing with my best friend on the playground, or why he hated Yonnie. Then he leaned in close to my face and said, "If I ever see or even hear tell of you playing with or associating with any nigger ever again I am going to have to whip your ass and burn a cross in little Yonnie's yard to make you understand. Do you want me to burn a cross in her yard, Jvonne?"

I was crying so hard now that snot was running down my face. I stammered, "No, sir." I had seen crosses burned symbolically during the drunken parties and I knew it meant something scary. The next day at school would change the rest of my school days, forever. When I saw Yonnie, I didn't just feel happy to see her anymore; I felt afraid. I replayed the warning from my dad in my head. So, I began to ignore and avoid her, even as it broke my little heart.

At first she still tried to be as we were but since I was so aloof I suppose she eventually stopped trying and I went inside myself a little and felt very sad. She had no way of knowing I was just trying to protect her from my daddy's violence, which I was starting to see more and more frequently, especially on the weekends. Those weekends degraded and degenerated fast! There were Klan rallies, cross burnings, being dragged around to other people's houses for drunken parties until the p.m. hours turned to the a.m. hours of the morning. On one occasion I even walked into a kitchen to see a tableful of people passing around a needle and shooting up. There were always so many people and such loud music that I would crawl behind the couch of whosever house we were at and try to get some sleep.

By 1st grade, my dad had my mom sew me a little miniature KKK robe, so he could proudly parade me around as a little beacon of his hate-filled indoctrination. Even though it was not what was in my authentic heart, for my dad and his approval I wore it and tried to assimilate the attitude he expected of me. Once, while at a huge rally in Stone Mountain, Georgia, the local news showed up and there was a ruckus because one of the cameramen was black. The Klansmen surrounded the news van and wouldn't let him out to do his job. I honestly don't even remember how that ended but I think they got someone else to do the filming.

Meanwhile, at school, I had no friends at all. We had a decent ratio of black students that I had to avoid like the plague so as not to anger my dad, and of course if any of my white friends were playing with the black children I couldn't play with them anymore either. I suppose other children started to wonder what was wrong with me but there was no way to explain it. I wasn't allowed to join Girl Scouts like I wanted to because as my dad put it, "No daughter of mine is going to go camping with a bunch of niggers!" I wasn't allowed to be a cheerleader at school because "No way are you going to cheer on a bunch of niggers!" So, my aspirations to successfully integrate into my peer group were stunted from the get-go.

By 2nd grade, and seven years old, I was falling asleep in class due to the fact that the alcohol-fueled way of life at home had started to spill into weekdays as well. Hatred and violence had turned criminal in ways that scar a child's mind forever. On the first occasion that I was present for such violence I was told to lay down on the back floorboard of our family car. My dad was instructing my mom to hold the steering wheel. The next thing I heard was a barrage of gunfire out the driver's side window. I was so scared but curious and I rose up in time to see that my dad was riddling someone's car with multiple bullets. A little "message," as my dad called it!

On the second occasion that I was present for his criminal exploits I was again told to lay down on the back floorboard, Mom again instructed to hold the steering wheel. This time I rose just in time to see that my dad was holding a glass soda bottle with a rag sticking out the top that he lit on fire and threw like a bomb through someone's front window. I actually saw their curtains go up in flames. I would overhear in a conversation he had with others later that it had been the home of a young white woman who had a black baby. If I had been afraid of my dad before, let me tell you I was terrified now. As far as my belief went, my dad just might murder someone if they crossed him.

In 3rd grade, by now age eight, they started a six-week square dancing program in physical education class. I refused to touch the hands of the three black boys in our class when they would pass my way. The P.E. teacher was livid! She yelled at me to go sit in the hallway and wait for her. I was so scared I went back to my classroom and hid under my desk. After P.E. was over she tracked me down and told me matter-of-factly that if I did not participate fully the next day that she would paddle me. Now I was getting it from both sides. She would paddle me if I didn't dance with the black boys and my dad would punish me severely if I did.

That day after school I told my dad what I was going to have to do. He started drinking and loaded my mom and me up in the car. We drove back to the school and marched into the office. He told the principal that he was the Grand Dragon of the KKK and no daughter of his would be dancing with niggers! The two of them came to an arrangement, whereby I sat in the principal's office those entire six weeks of P.E. and wrote sentences while my peers danced and developed normally.

Finally, at home a new age was dawning, one that would lesson my dad's presence around the house. He began to cheat on my mom, so he no longer wanted us along for his weekend exploits. Personally, I was relieved! As far as I was concerned he could just stay gone, but my mother was emotionally broken at the mere thought of being without him; she had no life beyond my dad. She was absolutely and completely in love with the man. In her own words: "The sun rose and set in his asshole"!

One Friday night when my dad was getting ready to leave, my mom couldn't bear it. She wanted to be wherever he was even if that was riding shotgun to some horrible crime spree. I was in the living room watching TV when I heard a ruckus in the hallway. I peeped around the corner and saw my mom standing in front of my dad, begging him not to go. He was trying to get around her. She started pounding on his chest, crying, "Please don't leave me, I love you!" I'm not sure if he pushed her down, or she lost her footing because he kept advancing forward, but she fell back onto the ground. As she landed on her back he whipped a loaded pistol out of his pocket and cocked it in her face.

Time froze it seemed, long enough for me to remember that there was a weapon rack in the living room that held many guns, knives, swords and the like. I bolted up on the back of the couch and grabbed a long machete, then flew to my mom's side and nervously spoke up in her defense. "If you kill my mommy, then I will kill you!" I told him. I think it snapped him out of it momentarily, long enough to respond out of some sort of freakish pride in me for embracing violence because he half-smiled, half-smirked then casually replaced the gun in his pocket and left. My mother lay there in a ball on the floor, crying.

This would become my new weekend ritual, sitting on the couch, trying to watch TV, with my mom laying her head in my eight-year-old lap, crying *all* weekend with me petting her head and face while she asked me questions like, "Jvonne, why do you think your daddy doesn't love me anymore" or statements like, "I've been a good and loyal wife. I've done everything he ever asked . . . oh Jvonne, he doesn't love me anymore," followed by the sort of heartbroken wailing that only a dying animal could muster. I'll admit, although I didn't realize it at the time, this was the beginning of when I started to lose respect for my mother. In my little mind, with only two horribly dysfunctional examples of how human beings conduct themselves during a crisis, it was my mom who worried me most. Why? Because she accepted being a victim. She wore it like a crown. She clung to it. Embraced it and wouldn't let it go. She was sad all the time. My advice to her at eight years old sent her into even deeper wailing than before. "Why don't you just leave the son of a bitch?" I asked. "Oh Jvonne, how could you say that, he's your daddy, I love him" . . . blah, blah, blah, blah, became all I heard. As the end of my mom and dad as a couple drew closer, there would be a few more traumatic experiences to scar my mind, one of which I remember as the scariest to my personal safety.

My mom had begun to take what I guess for her was a proactive approach to my dad's cheating. Instead of lying on the couch crying all weekend we now rode up and down the roads all over the county trying to catch him in the act. I was just glad to be out of the house, mostly because my dad had shattered any hopes of safety there. He would actually tell us before he left, "You better keep the lights out, and crawl from room to room so no one sees your shadow, or you might get your head blown off. I've got a lot of enemies and they might mistake you for me." Then he would leave us unprotected all weekend. We would literally sit in the dark and crawl back and forth to the bathroom when we needed to use it. So yeah, riding the roads was preferable to that! Not to mention every once in a while Mom would spare a quarter for me to ride one of those horse machines that used to be outside all grocery stores. I remember on one occasion the horse got stuck on a quarter and just kept going and going and going. In my mind I pretended I was riding to California to marry Richie Cunningham from the TV show *Happy Days*.

On another occasion my dad spotted us in town before we spotted him. All I can imagine is he became angry at being looked for. It was 1 a.m. and Mom had just driven through a fast food joint to get me a sausage and egg biscuit. She had the car facing the main road in hopes of seeing him go by. However, he came into the parking lot from the rear behind us and rammed his car into the back of ours. He got out yelling for her to get her ass home! She complied and he drove behind us, dangerously close to her back bumper all the way home. When we were almost there, he whipped around us like a mad man and pulled into the driveway first. When we pulled up he was already leaning against the hood of his car, with a shotgun in hand. I did not want to get out of the car. I believed he was going to kill us both. My mom coaxed me out, saying he would never hurt me, but the minute we were both out he shot a huge tree branch out of a nearby tree and it fell really close to us. I screamed and ran into the house.

They argued in the kitchen for a while then he just went to bed, not caring that sleep for anyone else would be impossible after trauma like that. My bowels were in a tizzy and I needed so badly to use the bathroom but the only bathroom was right next to his bedroom. My mom tried once more to convince me that he would never hurt me so that I would go use the bathroom, but after that tree branch episode with the shotgun I didn't believe it. So, she got me an empty lard canister and I sat on it on the kitchen floor to defecate.

One Sunday afternoon, she and I returned home from one of our "looking for him" sprees, only to find him already there. It was midafternoon and when she saw his car in the driveway she got excited, thinking he had come home early to her. However, as we opened the front door and walked in the greeting we received was hearing the sound and movement of him pumping a pump shotgun from his sitting place on the couch, with beer in hand. A pile of my mother's clothes lay in the middle of the living room floor. "You have an hour to get out before I unload this into you," he told her. She began to cry and bustle around getting things together. She told me to get just a few things that were important to me, but before I did I first went to my room and came out with the ridiculous child-sized confederate hat he had always made me wear to Klan rallies. I threw it at him and told him to give it to his "little boy," as Mom and I had learned his lover had a small male child from a previous relationship.

I went outside and started filling the car with my calico cat and the entire litter of kittens she had recently had. My mom came out and told me I couldn't possibly take all those cats because she had no idea where we were even going to go. I could only take one, so I put the mama cat and all but one of her kittens back. I held onto that one little kitten like it was my life and then went over to say goodbye to my grandparents. Life had ceased to be beautiful long ago, but now I was losing my home, my closeness to my grandparents and my favorite little cousin and playmate Kaylee, who lived on the other side of them. Once in the car, my mom cried all the way to her sister's house, which was a thirty-minute drive. I can't really remember all of what I was thinking and feeling save one thing: my dad had finally succeeded in teaching me hate. The first person I ever truly hated in my life was him.

Not I

Don't put your lifelong pain on me, or tell me what
I will, or will not be
I've watched you suffer, I've watched you cry
Took care of you, while my insides died
A little woman, and a little girl
At a man's mercy, in a man's world
From loneliness, there stemmed such grief
You made bad judgements, beyond belief
I've watched you suffer, I've watched you cry
From being my mother, to living a lie
I, the child would soon grow up
Believing that love, was never enough
Understanding that pain, was all that we shared
But once you moved on, you no longer cared
I've watched you suffer, I've watched you cry
But when it was my turn, you left me to die
At a man's mercy, in a man's world
Broken and scared, still just a girl
With only myself, no one to console me
Battered and used, by the ones who did hold me
I've watched you suffer, I've watched you cry
Never for me, not one tear in your eye
The misplaced little girl, grew up too fast
The time for her mother, had already passed
When the woman would call her, still she would come
Help, hold, console her, all the while numb

I've watched you suffer, I've watched you cry
Until there were no tears, left for you in my eyes
Still yet I've loved you, it feels very strange
Like loving your torment, or adoring your pain
I cling to the freedom, of being myself
I am not like you, don't need anyone else
I've watched you suffer, I've watched you cry
Then I walked away slowly, saying: Not I

CHAPTER 2

Mother, Martyr, Stranger

AFTER A BRIEF STAY WITH one of her sisters, Mom rented us a basement apartment in town. I was nine years old. I know my dad destroyed her heart, but she would in time destroy mine. The first thing she taught me as a woman was how to disrespect yourself completely. Following her divorce from my dad she went through a barrage of men. It started with a one-night stand with a man she had just met in the parking lot of a fast food chain restaurant. For that one, there was nowhere for me to be except lying on the floor beside the motel room bed where they were having sex. I remember being scared of the weird noises I could hear her making in the dark.

Then there was a college boy that came over to the apartment twice to "shower" with her. After a couple of fleeting hookups, she was ready to have a live-in lover. Much to my dismay, she met one at the jail where she worked as a janitor. No, not a deputy, or coworker; I mean, she literally met a man who was in the jail she had to clean. Apparently, he whistled at her from behind bars and set her heart aflutter! This man moved in with us as soon as he got out of jail.

Several months later when that didn't work out, she moved his nineteen-year-old younger brother in and for a time they were lovers. Crazy thing about that one was, I felt like I had a big brother. Alas, she didn't keep him either. Instead, she met another man who was not only in jail when she met him but had even been to prison. He would become my first stepdad, and father of my sister.

They called him Button and he was a skinny, wiry little man. Turns out, he too was an alcoholic, just of a different variety. His drunkenness had stages; he was moody and broody when he wasn't drinking, happy and likeable when he would first start drinking and then as it went along he would become argumentative and spiteful in his words, actions and deeds. He hid bottles of liquor in strange places—under boards in the floor, under the bathroom sink, behind the cleaning supplies, etc. My dad had always been a beer-fueled weekend drunk, one who made a choice week after week to repeat the same behavior. As for my stepdad, I got the feeling he was sick and incapable of not drinking. He had a sister die of cirrhosis of the liver because alcoholism ran so rampant in his family. Of course, with that said, he too continued to taint my life with further dysfunction and at times I was scared of him, not because he was ever physically violent, but he sure was mean by way of spiteful words and actions.

For example, once when Button was happy drunk he put a tire swing up in a tree for me, which was awesome. I would go outside with my boom box and swing for hours from that tree. Then several months later, when he and my mom had argued over something, he went outside and chopped it down. He never put it back up. I guess the worst thing he did was make life further unstable and insecure. He liked to focus on me as a source of strife between he and my mother, but then step-parents who aren't alcoholics often do that too. As usual he fulfilled my mom's pattern of being a man who would not hold a job. She supported him as she had done my father and her two live-in lovers in between. I must admit though, every once in a while, Button was funny without meaning to be. Once while living in a small trailer we were renting I was lying over the living room heat vent trying to warm up before bed. Button, drinking, yelled from the kitchen, "Will you stop hogging all the damn heat! The rest of us need to be warm too."

I was eleven when my mom became pregnant with my sister. We had been living in a trailer park but were in the middle of a move to an old farmhouse where Button was to be caretaker of the property. I had gone to say goodbye to a little girl that I had played with and protected from a group of rascally kids in the park. She and I had just walked to the pond in the center of the park, when the group of brats (who were a mix of brothers, sisters and cousins) surrounded us. The boy who led the pack began to taunt me. We had words. He then approached me and my friend threateningly, so I pushed him down to the ground, took my friend's hand and started to run for home. Over my shoulder, I heard him call me a chicken and I made the sad mistake of turning around to go back.

When his clenched hand made contact with the side of my head and into my left eye, I knew immediately something was severely wrong. My vision went instantaneously double and I began throwing up bile. He had smashed me with a rock and as I stumbled for home I had never been so sick to my stomach. My vision was blurry, double and distorted. For a month, I was treated for a scratch across the cornea by my regular doctor, but the double vision would not go away. He sent me to an eye specialist who from a CAT scan found that my left eye socket was broken. The muscles and nerves had fallen into the broken gap and were being pinched as the bone tried to grow back together. A blowout fracture they called it, and so I was scheduled for emergency surgery at a children's hospital that was a hundred miles away. My mom had given birth to my sister during that month of trial and error by my medical doctor and had to leave her with Button's family to make the trip.

The cruelest part of the whole thing was how even though the hospital had put her and my stepdad up in a Ronald McDonald house for free, my mother was not allowed to spend very much time with me per my stepdad. When she was with me she was anxious to get back to him at all times. The morning of my surgery I lay awake, scared and alone, wondering when my mom would get there, so when the room door swung open at 6 a.m. that morning, I called out "Mom?" Oddly enough, it was my dad who walked through the door. He was remarried now. My stepmom was the woman he had cheated on my mom with. He was also at one of those points where he was "trying" not to drink. He had borrowed gas money from a preacher to be there that morning and although my mom did run in at the last minute to see me off to surgery I will always remember that it was my severely absentee father who was there that morning.

I had to wear an eye patch for six months over that eye while it healed, with the possibility of a second surgery looming. At school, cruel kids would taunt me with words like "pirate" and "one eye." I found it incredibly hurtful to be made fun of for something that I could not help. I had been warned that I could not take another hit to that eye or I could lose it, so I took the taunts and went on with my head down. That same year, I developed a condition known as spastic bladder. Every time I went to urinate it would feel like I couldn't get it all out and it would burn afterwards. The doctor explained it as a nervous condition and put me on a medicine that turned my pee blue! Between the constant arguing that went on at home between my mom and stepdad, along with the cruelty coming at me from school classmates, apparently my bladder would just tighten up and spasm. I didn't much understand it. All I knew was it was extremely painful.

By 8th grade and age thirteen, Button had left my mom and sister behind. They divorced and he was never part of our lives again. My sister was just two years old. I've tried to tell her over the years that she was the lucky one: at least he split and didn't keep hurting, confusing and disappointing her. Meanwhile my dad would do nothing but. Whenever I got to see or spend time with my dad it was almost always guaranteed dysfunction. Once, while on a weekend visit with him he made me help him steal a bunch of hanging flower baskets from a florist in the dead of the night, so he could sell them at the flea market the next morning. On another occasion he and a drunk friend of his wanted to go spotlight deer. My dad was not a hunter. He used his guns to terrorize people, but had a soft spot for animals. As I sat squeezed between these two drunk rednecks in the front seat of a pickup truck with my dad holding the spotlight out the passenger window, a deer did in fact come into view. My dad looked at me, winked and acted like he dropped the light on the floorboard before his friend could take the shot. Every now and then I would see a glimmer of good in the bad man's eye.

By this point in my life we had already lived in twenty-one places, all within the same county, all substandard dumps. My mom was forty, with a two-year-old, and had gotten onto welfare so that she wouldn't ever have to go back to work. She had been diagnosed with a strange condition called fibromyalgia and often complained of extreme physical pain and chronic tiredness. She was for the time without a man, and as usual we lived in poverty. One of the ways that both my mom and dad had supplemented poverty for years and years was to be thieves. My dad was a dumpster diver. He would also steal flowers and lawn statues from people's yards and gardens, then sell them at the flea market.

My mom was a grocery and department store shoplifter. Anything we couldn't afford had been going in her purse for years. I knew this because from age seven on, she had always made me stand on the end of the buggy with my back to her to block the view of others. I don't know how she ever figured she was fooling me; I could hear the unzip and zip back up of her purse. I knew what she was doing. When I confronted her with it, all that changed was I didn't have to turn around on the end of the buggy any more; instead I would face her and be the lookout for anyone coming up behind her. When I started carrying my own purse, around the age of ten, she would use it also to get double the stuff. By then I had the idea that, wow, if you want anything just take it!

It was during one of these grocery store excursions that I met up with my mom in the center of the store so she could load up my purse with toothpaste, shampoo and aspirin. We then bought what little she could afford on food stamps and went towards the car. As we exited the store the manager came running after us. He told her we needed to come back inside. I saw the look on her face—like a deer caught in headlights. She was scared. Oddly enough he didn't seem to suspect her at all. We sat in his office with me thinking we were both in trouble. He asked only me to open and empty my purse. I was crying as my mother said things to me in front of the manager to make herself look as if she were shocked and could not understand why or how her little girl would do such a thing. He told her that I was never allowed to come back to his store. He let us go and with her purse still full of stolen goods we left. In the car she thanked me for being smart enough not to rat her out.

Without a man to obsess over, my mom became all about my baby sister. Her method of dealing with me, was not to. Meaning by age thirteen, I had absolute freedom. I came and went as I pleased, hardly ever mentioned where I was going, was never asked when I'd be back. I thought it was great! We moved into a house right in town, one street over from my paternal grandma who had also moved to town. My grandpa passed away that year and I was incredibly sad because he was the only person in my life who had never hurt me, not with words, actions or deed. So that summer, because grandma was having a hard time coping with the loss, my favorite cousin Kaylee spent the entire summer at her house, which meant I had a buddy! My cousin and I would head out at sunrise on our bicycles and ride all day long. We would ride to the park and play and then we would ride to the lake and swim for a while. Afterwards we would ride around the whole county all day long having fun. It was nothing to log twenty to thirty miles a day. I can honestly say that was the best summer of my life during childhood.

I loved physical fitness. I dreamed of being a P.E. teacher someday. When night would fall, I would go home from a full day of bike riding and spend the last hour or so before bed dancing about my room. I loved activity! During those hot summer days, my cousin and I would often stop at this convenience store in the middle of town for drinks when we got thirsty and snacks if we could afford them. She knew the cashier by first name because she had been stopping in there for years with her mom. The cashier was a forty-four-year-old man named Fred, who was extremely friendly. I remember commenting to my cousin what a nice man he was. He sometimes, knowing we had no money, would say the soda pop or snack was on him.

Summer passed and my cousin had to go back home. It would be just me biking my days away now. As I headed out alone on one such occasion I noticed a man across the street with the hood of his car up. As I passed by on my bicycle, he whistled at me, which I thought was gross since he was a grown man and also because he had a bandanna tied around his head and looked dirty. I just pedaled on by fast!

Later that evening, around suppertime when I went home, there that man sat on the couch with my mom, which might've been funny if it wasn't so damn sad. My mom introduced him as Wade and announced he was staying for dinner. So, I just grabbed a snack and left. I was riding my bike two streets over when someone called my name. It was Paul, the old boyfriend of my mom's from when I was ten, the one I had felt was like an older brother. We talked for a while. Ironically, he lived that close by, so we started hanging out in the evenings. My biking turned to long walks with Paul. We climbed on top of the roofs of local businesses, just for shits and giggles. Or we would hang out at the playground in the dead of night, him pushing me wildly on the merry-go-round.

Then one night on one of our walks, something strange happened. He pointed out to me that the old man from the convenience store, Fred, lived in a house one street over from mine. We hid behind some bushes and "spied" on Fred as he sat on his front porch drinking something. Stuck behind that bush, waiting for Fred to go in was getting rather boring, so I told Paul I was leaving. He stood up with me and we just started running down the middle of the street laughing. Then came a heavy, scudding sound. Something metal was making contact with the street at a pretty fast pace. We both shrieked and jumped out of the way of a very long, very heavy, fast-moving flashlight. "What the hell!" Paul exclaimed and I asked, "Where did that come from?" We looked back up the street; Fred had gone back into his house. Paul was mad. He immediately concluded that Fred had thrown the flashlight at us. "Why would he do that?" I asked. "Let's go see," said Paul. We walked back to Fred's house and Paul knocked on the door with me standing behind him. Fred came to the door, looking sheepish as Paul confronted him. Fred admitted to throwing the flashlight, but I still wanted to know why! I had just turned fourteen, and I suppose I must've been very naive because even after he tried to explain, I didn't fully get it. He said he just saw us together and felt overwhelmed and then he apologized and shut the door. I still didn't understand, but Paul evidently did and when he tried to explain it to me I didn't really believe it. He said obviously Fred had a "thing" for me! My response was very teenaged girl: *What? Yuck! What? No!*

After just three weeks of dinners, Mom moved Wade the bandanna man in with us. *Good Lord,* I thought. *How lonely and desperate is this woman?* As I mentioned earlier, it was customary for me to go from bike riding all day to my room to play music and dance at night. One night my mom came into my room, turned the music down and told me Wade was watching TV and wanted me to cut the volume of my music down. I pointed out several things to her, like how in a year's time she had never had an issue of that sort with my music when she was watching TV, or how if he wasn't happy he could go home and also how I didn't really care what he wanted. A bit smart mouth maybe, but trust me I was really tired of this routine. She went out and I cut the music back up and resumed my activities. Then my bedroom door opened again and it was Wade himself with my mom behind him. He reached for the knob of my stereo and turned it down. I told him not to touch my stuff and turned it back up. He turned it down. I turned it up. Then he grabbed me in a headlock, sat on my bed with me on his lap and spanked me brutally hard (in fact a handprint bruise remained on my gluteal flesh for over two weeks). I fought free and, crying uncontrollably not from physical pain so much as feeling violated and extremely angry, I told him he had just made the biggest mistake of his life. I went to the phone and called my violent, gun-toting, alcoholic dad.

My dad was living one county over, about a thirty-minute drive, but when he answered and I told him through tears what had happened, he was there in like fifteen. Now make no mistake, I knew my dad; my protection was secondary only to his chance to show his violent streak of terror and retribution. I really didn't care so long as he showed up, which he did, with shotgun in hand of course. When he arrived he knocked on the storm door with the barrel of the gun and the glass shattered. Wade hid behind my mom who was holding my baby sister. I glared at him with satisfaction and made mention of how his manliness didn't seem to extend past beating teenage girls. Then I left with my dad and stepmom.

They took me just one street over to my grandma's house. My stepmom took pictures of my butt bruises and we went to the police. Wade was charged with assault and arrested, which made me feel safe enough to go back the next day to get my stuff. It had been decided I would live with my grandma until the school year was over. When I arrived to get my stuff, my mother looked at me like she had never hated someone so much. It hurt so bad inside that she would stand for a virtual stranger to assault her daughter that way. I tried to silently go about getting my things but she wanted to accost me verbally about how I had sabotaged her happiness. Then, as if knowing what meant the most to me in that room, she just started tearing my Cyndi Lauper posters off the wall. I pushed on her arms to try and stop her destroying my things. She slapped my face and without thinking I instinctively slapped her back. It was ugly. She pushed me out the front door and dragged me by the foot down the porch and I kicked at her with my high-heeled boot which pierced her arm. As she started to bleed I just got up and ran away crying back to my grandma's house.

Ah, my poor grandma. She was an anxiety-riddled woman who worried constantly about everything. She was obsessively negative and always thought she was dying from something or other. She had been the sixteen-year-old child bride of my grandpa when he was a thirty-seven-year-old man! She had three babies die before birthing three more that lived. She had never "really been right since," so the story goes. My point is she really wasn't capable of dealing with me. She complained that I used too much water taking daily showers. She complained that I used too much toilet paper when I went to the bathroom and she really complained about my not being inside the house for the night by 6 p.m. I realized she was old but I found it impossible to fathom being in that early, since my routine had been to stay out until 9 or 10 on weekdays, 11 or 12 midnight on weekends. I guess I don't have to tell you there was no way for it to work out and so my dad came back and took me home with him. I had to change schools; I was in 9th grade at the time.

Since I was moving to another county, I went to say goodbye to Fred at the convenience store. I was so emotionally upset by all that had happened between my mom and me that I started to cry as I explained he wouldn't be seeing me stop in on my bike anymore. Oddly enough, he held me, patted my back and told me everything would be okay. Then I left to see what life with my dad, stepmom and stepbrother would be like.

"Family"

We're not normal people, waiting on normal things
We're dysfunctional white trash, waiting to see what cha-
os brings
We're not happy together, there is no hearth and home
We're just clinging to each other, because we're afraid to
be alone
We're not what I call family, we throw each other under
the bus
We're in this shit together, but really there is no love
We're not meant to make it, statistically born to fail
We're just a bunch of degenerates, living inside a self-
made Hell
We're not big "Billy" badass, just because we talk such shit
We're a bunch of fucking lowlifes, if you want the truth of it
We're the dregs upon the system, the boil on the ass of life
We're family until the time comes, to insert the backside
knife

CHAPTER 3

Dragging it Around

BEFORE WE DELVE INTO WHAT life back with my dad turned into, let me pause here to fill in some gaps. Mostly, just a larger look at what I was going through at school while living through all the aforementioned at home.

Back in 2008, when Facebook started becoming the big deal and Myspace was trending out, the first person I searched for on Facebook was Yonnie. My lost, long ago friend from kindergarten that my dad had threatened me about all those years ago. I never found her. I reconnected with a bunch of ex-classmates however from grade through high school. Why? I wanted to hear their version of events and their impressions of me from that era. I was trying to collect more perspective, outside perspective if you will, for this part of my book . . . which tells you how long writing this book has been in my head, even before the reality of it. In fact, I openly told ex-classmates that interacted with me there that I was writing a book about my life. I remember this one guy—who back in middle school I thought was a hateful little shit and a badass wannabe—asking me why I would want to drag this kind of shit up anyway? It was a good question, and not one that I could answer easily. The answer wasn't clear to me so much even then, but I could no doubt answer him now: I didn't want to "drag it up." The truth is I wasn't dragging anything *up*, but I was dragging it around like a dead corpse, in that it was heavy and quite the burden to "drag around." I guess I thought if I wrote about it, perhaps I could purge it and be done with it. So, respect it fella, if you will, as to why I had to tell my story: in order to ever be able to stop "dragging it around."

Ah, old school days! It deserves its own chapter for the tragedy that it was in its own right. I had no friends at all by the time I hit 2nd grade. I was seven years old and I was deep in, two strong years of constant at-home indoctrination. My dad had begun to tell me awful things about black people. Things that if you are seven years old and in 2nd grade, you believe, especially if either of your parents are the ones telling you. You are looking to them for guidance, to help shape your world view so that hopefully you grow up nice and balanced. How could you possibly know at age seven that your father was teaching you wrong things? I mean, I knew they felt wrong. I knew I hesitated in my own little mind to believe such nonsense, but in the end my home life and its resident terrorist—my father—won out for a little while.

He told me blacks carried diseases that could be caught just by accidentally touching their skin and that if one ever even bumped into me I should immediately go wash that part of my body. I started to develop nervous anxiety and issues of acting out of that nervous anxiety. I'm sure teachers wondered what was wrong with me. I can remember running to the bathroom to scrub my arm from wrist to shoulder, just because a little black boy brushed his arm against mine in our passing at the water fountain.

By age eight and 3rd grade, during a practice session of our whole class acting out the Nutcracker for a Christmas play, one little girl (black) had gone to the bathroom during a break. As we were about to start back up another student tried to tell the teacher that the little girl wasn't back yet, to which I promptly retorted, "We don't need niggers in our play anyway." I was ousted by the teacher from the whole thing and made to sit out alone while the show went on. I know she did the right thing, but I still find it sad that even today, teachers have such limited time to educate a large group of children that they can't focus too much on why a kid is acting out a certain way. All they know is it's disruptive. I would agree, because from my standpoint it was extremely disruptive to my proper growth as a child to be raised by a hate-filled criminal, but that was my reality at the time.

Where the play was concerned, I had hopes that I might at least get to control the light switch on the actual day of the program. The teacher had told me I could. However, the day of the play came and by then a little black boy had acted out in some way to get himself ousted from the play and as I neared the light switch to take up my duty he was already sitting by it, shaking his head *no!* I shrunk back to my seat. I guess it was what they call karma, only I didn't know that term then. It felt right though, for him to do the lights, after all I had in one fell swoop insulted a whole race. The irony was not completely lost on me.

Of course, you know what happened in 4th grade—my dad making a complete ass out of he and I both over the square-dancing dilemma in P.E. Thankfully by 5th grade my mom and dad were divorced and he was not a constant presence in my life. Now we could just move on into the extremely confused phase of my childhood. Nearing ten years old, with the threat of 5th grade looming over my head, I just wanted to enjoy the summer of 1983. I had a bicycle and a little am/fm transistor radio with headphones. I'm sure that sounds boring as hell to the modern-day kid but for this little blond-headed redneck child both were a Godsend. Bicycling always felt like freedom to me, even at such a young age. You could hop on your bicycle and drive away from the things at home that hurt you. You could breeze along the sidewalk with your arms outstretched while feeling the wind on your face and just pedal until all your worries faded away. The radio helped facilitate this further. Music is a distraction at its worst and a transformative healer at its best. It was on one of those sunny summer days while gliding along as described, the country music station hum drumming on about something, when my bike wheel hit an uneven bump in the sidewalk. I lurched forward a bit to keep from wrecking and it was such a hard bump my radio changed stations.

But wait . . . what was this incredible sound coming through my radio now? The sad twang of the only genre of music I had ever known was gone and in its place was this strong female voice and she was singing about girls just wanting to have fun. I thought, *Yeah, I'm a girl. I just want to have fun.* What is this, I wondered? You must remember, all I had ever been exposed to was country music and I mean no disrespect to country music when I say it was one of the best days of my little life when I discovered the sound of rock 'n' roll! I would *never* turn the dial again. It was set to this station that my mom would later have to explain to me was Rock & Roll. I dare say it was my savior of sorts, symbolic of a much greater freedom than the temporary riding of a bike could provide.

I wondered who that woman was singing that really cool song and would just listen to the radio all day waiting to hear that song play. Then one night that same summer, God gave me another gift. I was sitting up late—it was a Friday night, which meant I was watching *Gunsmoke*. Remember when there were only three channels on TV? Add being poverty-stricken poor and cable is out of the question, so yeah, three channels. Well, as fate would have it right in the middle of *Gunsmoke* the channel went to complete fuzz. I was so darn mad that I was going to have to get up and screw with the antenna and flip the channels to try to bring it back into focus. Except when I changed the channel there was that voice again. It was singing something different but it was the same voice, I just knew it. When I got my first glimpse of Cyndi Lauper in the "Time After Time" video that was playing that night on a show called *Friday Night Videos*, I was instantly in awe! Her flame-red hair with checkerboarded shaved side, her exotic and wild-looking makeup and clothes excited my little mind. It was such a stunning visual. It made me feel warm and fuzzy on the inside, like everything could be all right. It made me feel like a kid at the fair or the circus taking in all the bright colors. Her voice simultaneously angelic and strong, then squeaky and loud; I loved it!

I probably drove a few people crazy with the whole Cyndi Lauper bit. Like the girl in 5th grade who, while we were on a field trip to the park had me stalking her around the tennis courts because she was carrying around a boom box playing "Girls Just Want to Have Fun." However, both Cyndi's music and her look were giving me confidence that there was more to life than just the dribs and drabs. There had to be! That year when we were told to do book reports and come to school dressed as the main character, I asked the teacher if I could do mine on Cyndi Lauper. She told me regretfully no, it had to be a character from a real book. I ended up being Goldilocks of three bears fame for that damn report! My mom had told me, however, that if it was that important to me she would allow me to go on the last day of school dressed as Cyndi Lauper. Oh boy, something to look forward to.

Back in my time at grade school we had what were called pods: three classrooms all in the same wide space divided only by bulletin-type boards. The layout was open and you could hear the other two teachers teaching their students even as yours tried to teach you. I'm glad they changed that dynamic in public education. On the last day of school, I was so excited that morning. I had makeup all over my face, done up wild Cyndi style. I had thrift shop clothes that I had assembled quite the outfit from, and some temporary spray in red color for my hair. I spent so much time dressing up, I was running towards my pod almost late as the bell rang. It made for quite the entrance, even though it wasn't planned. When I came through the opening of that three-class-room pod, a ripple effect of sorts started with one kid, then two, elbowing others to look and before thirty seconds could elapse, that entire pod—some sixty plus children—laughed at me all at the same time. Oh, it was daunting, scary even, but at the same time they were finally laughing and poking fun at me on my terms because of something I chose to do instead of the same ole pickings on about being poor, or being weird, or having "cooties," or just general avoidance of me because of how I had acted out for two years before, under the daily onslaught of my father's angry and often violent presence. A new time was dawning, one where I planned on being more in control of the why's and what for's that people had for either avoiding me or making fun of me.

Next came middle school. A time when children start becoming young adults. What used to just be a large group of children suddenly started dividing up into groups: the jocks, the preps, the rednecks, the nerds, the outcasts and then me. Yes, even the outcasts could not be my group because they became the ones who experimented with drugs, alcohol and promiscuous sex, none of which I wanted any part of. So, I just didn't fit in anywhere it seemed. I was often disregarded and always chosen last for everything whether it be team sports or just partnering up by twos for projects. Even other kids who might not be popular avoided me. I would be lying if I claimed it didn't hurt on the inside, but what was on the inside I guarded like a lion. On the outside, I fronted like I didn't really give a shit. I didn't just front; if confronted in an aggressive manner by someone, be it male or female, I would more often than not just knock the hell out of them. I didn't start fights; I tried to keep to myself, but there will always be bullies and assholes, even amongst children. What they often found underneath my weird Cyndi Lauper—clad exterior was a pent-up anger that would finish whatever sort of shit they wished to start.

Case in point: in 7th grade an obnoxious boy with a loud motor mouth wouldn't stop making fun of me during P.E. class. He had been going on for about ten minutes straight with his demeaning comments, hurtful words and painful jibes. When ignoring him didn't work, I just turned my bow and arrow on him (we were practicing archery in P.E.). I told him if he didn't shut his chubby little jowls, I might just put my arrow through his face! He shut up, quick. I think because people didn't really know me they weren't sure if I might not do some shit like that, which is exactly what I wanted them to think because it kept them off of and away from me.

School wasn't all bad though, because I loved to learn. English, reading and writing were always my favorite subjects and in 7th grade for the first time in my life I got to join a club. It was called the Young Authors Club, and we even had a small print journal published school wide. I wrote a lot of poetry. All my life writing—poetry in particular—served as a tool for me to express myself. Often, I would be so busy trying to survive my life I wouldn't know how I truly felt about something until a poem popped out of me and I read it back to myself. It always felt like what came to me to write was given to me from within by a force greater than myself. In fact, being a published writer was one of my first dreams for myself, that and being a P.E. teacher. It wasn't unusual for me to go through an entire school day never speaking a word to anyone other than my teachers. The teacher who headed the Young Authors Club was a wonderful lady who appreciated my writings so much that at the end of the school year, on awards day when all the students were gathered in the gymnasium to receive kudos, she acknowledged me. I was both elated and freaked out to walk up in front of over four hundred students to receive my honor, but it sure was nice. It wasn't the first time though, because earlier in the year, even with my knees feeling as if they would knock together and crumble, I had performed a lip sync of "True Colors" in the school-wide talent show. I had my imitation of Cyndi down so well, even the people who didn't like me clapped. Thanks Cyndi!

By 8th grade, however, I underwent an image change. I loved Cyndi and dressing like her was fun, but it wasn't hardcore enough. We were full-fledged teenagers now and with my late summer birthday I was usually the youngest in my class. People only had one of two ways that they affected me by then: either they made me nervous and scared or they just annoyed me constantly. It was time to widen the gap of "leave me the fuck alone," so I traded in my colorful duds and took on a completely black wardrobe, complete with bright red lipstick and nails. I didn't know there was a descriptive word for it—not sure there was one back then—but it was what by today's classification would be called gothic. Crucifixes hung around my neck in multiples. Chains around my waist, flat studs around my arms, leather jacket, leather boots. All I wanted to reflect was an edgy and a continuous "fuck you" to my peers in hopes they would all just leave me alone. Little did I know it would amp some of them up to a whole new level. The insults weren't so PG anymore. As a thirteen-year-old virgin girl it was a whole other level of hurtful when the chides turned from weirdo and freak to whore, slut and hooker! *Ah, what the hell, these people* I thought, so I just added fishnets and lace gloves to the ensemble. *Think what you will assholes,* I thought, *I will never change for anyone!*

It was that same year my grandpa Hubbard died. The hardest part about that was I had recently been saved and baptized in the small church I attended near our home. In that simple way that a child interprets scripture, I believed all I had to do was ask God and he would answer my prayers, right? So, when Grandpa got sick and was in the hospital, I prayed he would not die. When he died anyway, something broke in my heart that hurt so much I clung even further to anger and hostility as coping mechanisms. I found myself caught in a trap, one where I would take shit all day from peers at school and on the long bus ride home. Get home already angry and disgruntled, walk in and begin to eat ungodly amounts of food and sit and stew. My mom would ask what was wrong and I would just snap at her, then go lock myself in my room, or get out on my bicycle and ride for hours. My interchanges with my mom and baby sister were fraught with contention by day, then when they would go to sleep at night, I would sneak into their bedroom in the middle of the night just to watch them breathing. I remember thinking, *Please don't die and leave me, I love you,* but when a new day would start so would my meanness. My mom recently reminded me that she had once asked me back then why I was so hostile, and I had replied, "because it hurts to love and get close to people; all they do is leave. I protect my heart with anger."

Now I was fourteen and it was time to see what life back with my dad and his parental guidance would bring.

The Unseen

I am not this body, I am not this brain
I am not this hardship, I am not this pain
Inside I am eternal, inside I am dancing free
Trapped inside this body, is the spirit known as me
I have no race or color, I really have no name
Yet I am more important, every time I change
Closer to the creator, closer to the truth
Closer by inner knowing, that does not require proof
Whatever compels my waking, whatever compels my dreams
Is the same thing that compels me, to believe in The Unseen

CHAPTER 4

Knives, Eating Disorders and Hospitalization

LIVING WITH MY DAD AGAIN, after six years of him not really being a consistent part of my day-to-day life, was weird. He was on and off with the drinking, married to my stepmom, and had adopted her son. I had to share a room with my nine-year-old stepbrother until public housing could come through on a larger place for a family of four. I started a new school, and hoped not knowing anybody would be a good thing; maybe I'd even make some friends. Oh, it was okay for a couple of weeks. I even had a group of three girls that I ate lunch with every day. By now, though, I was what I was, socially speaking, and for the most part that meant introverted. Some people misunderstand the term 'introverted.' They think we're weird or strange or abnormal, and as teenagers, trust me, they never think about the reasons why a person is that way. So, just as I had three nice girls to eat lunch with, I also had three bullying type girls who would follow me down the hallways between class changes and kick me in the heels and back of the legs, trying to trip me up.

I tried avoidance but they always found me. I tried telling the guidance counselor, but she counseled me in a way that suggested it was my fault for dressing and being so weird. All that was left was telling my dad about it.

Of course, his solution was scary in and of itself. He handed me a very small—maybe three-inch—pocketknife and said, "Scratch them with this and they'll stop." Well, I still didn't like those odds: three girls and me with a joke of a knife in my pocket? I carried it, but never pulled it for like two weeks. After that I just left it at home because it didn't seem like the solution. However, the very day that I left it behind, one of the girls had a class with me, and a new student had come along that I think she was trying to show out for. She boasted that after class she was going to beat my ass.

Now, it only takes one major eye surgery for one to want to avoid fighting and it only takes being told you can't take another hit like that for one to feel nervous and scared to death when threatened with a beating. In my panic, I asked to go to the bathroom during class, but what I really did was go to the open door of the classroom where the one-and-only girl I had made solid friends with was having class. I waited till she looked up, motioned at her with my hall pass and waited as I heard her ask the teacher if she could go to the bathroom. We walked together to the bathroom to discuss my dilemma. I told her what I was being threatened with, then asked her, "Can you meet me after class and walk with me?" "I can," she said, "but I may be able to do better than that." She had known about my little "scratch" knife and had never really given an opinion on it. "Let me go back to class and I'll come get you in a few minutes," she said. We both went back to our classes and I sat, scared, wondering what she had in mind.

Almost at the end of the period I saw her waving for me to come out. That time I told the teacher I needed a drink of water. Once at the fountain my friend handed me a six-inch switchblade. When she demonstrated how it flew open I jumped back. I took it from her, held it, put it back in and flipped it out myself and thought, *Now this is a scary knife!* Immediately I envisioned pulling it out and popping it open in order to scare off the girl who wanted to harm me. Surely if someone saw this blade they would run for the hills just at the sight of it. I went back to class with this massive weapon and felt a little better about my chances of survival. However, when the bell rang I lagged behind, hoping the girl would get tired of waiting and move on without a confrontation. She did not. She was waiting for me in the hallway with the new student that she was trying to impress. I had the knife out, but closed, in my hand under my jacket. The rest is somewhat of a blur. She called me a foul name then drew her arm back with her fist balled up, ready to throw a punch at me. At that precise moment, I pulled the knife from my jacket, hit the switch and the blade came out just in time for her arm, mid-swing, to collide with the blade. There was this horrible five seconds that felt like forever where I drew the knife back, she screamed, the new student looked horrified, then we both screamed. The girl that I had cut bolted toward the office and I bolted in the opposite direction out the double doors, and ran away from the school.

Once I felt deep enough in the surrounding woods I put the still-open switchblade in my backpack and began to run for home. It was at least seven miles away! Two miles in I went into a convenience store and breathlessly asked to use the phone. I wanted to call my dad to come get me. The cashier acted funny and I became convinced that somehow she knew what I had done so I ran back out without making the phone call. About another half mile in I reached the main road and decided I should walk instead of run so it didn't look so damn suspicious. Then a cop car passed, hit the brakes and u-turned. I bolted again, but then I heard, "Freeze!" I turned to find two police officers—one male, one female—standing across the road from me and then two other police cars zoomed up. I was surrounded. I threw my backpack down and my hands up. To this day, I have no idea if they drew a gun on me or not but when you hear "Freeze!" you automatically assume so, even if you're just fourteen. They put me in the back of the police car, took my backpack and knife, drove me to the station and then they called my dad.

Once my dad showed up to the room they were holding me in he and my stepmother rushed in and started chiding me for what I had done. However, once the police stepped out the tone changed and my dad embraced me and said, "Good job." Good job? It sure didn't feel like a good job. It felt scary as hell. Was I going to prison? Was the girl all right? Did I get to go home? Anxiety was extremely high. The officers came back in and let my dad take me home. I was so shaken up my stepmom took me to the local mental health offices so I could see a counselor. The counselor recommended that I be checked into a nearby juvenile hospital facility.

At my first appearance in the juvenile court I was told I was suspended for the remainder of the school year and that since I was already checked into a facility it would be part of the probation I was placed on to complete the program per the resident doctor's orders. I would get my schooling there. In this hospital ward, I lived in a lockdown unit. There were about thirty kids in this program, all with various mental, emotional and behavioral problems. Each of us had our own hospital room. There were daily group therapy sessions, as well as weekly private sessions with the head psychiatrist. I spent three months on that unit where staff and the psychiatrist concluded that, amongst many problems, I was dealing with a full-blown eating disorder and so I was moved to the Eating Disorder unit which was right beside the juvenile unit. I spent another three months on that side. The truth is I did have an out-of-control eating disorder. The emotions that come with a true eating disorder are as intense for a 110-pound girl as they are for a 300-pound woman. Body image once distorted does not care if you are overweight or not because distorted body image is a problem of the mind. I wouldn't have been considered overweight even though my diagnosis was compulsive overeating disorder.

The problem was I thought about and obsessed over food throughout each and every day on a level that could only be described as abnormal. I would gorge myself with unusually large amounts of food. A lot of times it felt way beyond my control because unlike other types of addictions, like alcohol or drugs, you can't just cut all ties with food. The hospital used the same twelve steps for the eating disorder program that they use for Alcoholics Anonymous. We had to complete all twelve steps in order to be released. At the end, you got a coin with the serenity prayer, same as AA. I had been afflicted for quite some time with compulsive overeating disorder. I would eat unnecessarily huge amounts of food during times of stress and/or turmoil to try and comfort myself, whether I was hungry or not. I never purged this food; instead I would display further obsessive compulsive behavior to try and offset any potential weight gain. I would get right up from eating and go run laps around the outside of the house or I would literally be riding my bike while eating. I would sleep wrapped in a trash bag from the waist down, trying to sweat off pounds during the night while I slept. To give an example of one of my worst binges ever, I once ate half of a family-size lasagna, followed by two frozen pizzas, followed by three peanut butter and jelly sandwiches, followed by three ice cream bars!

During my stay at the hospital, my mother was called upon to come to family counseling sessions. She had since married Wade, the man who had beaten me. That complicated things. I missed my baby sister though. She was almost four now and I wanted to be back in her life. I missed her so much. Over the course of my stay at the hospital I decided to go back home with my mother once released. I would say I should've known better but even if I had stayed with my dad it was a lose-lose situation. My dad was angry with my decision to leave because he and my stepmom would be losing the monthly welfare check they had been collecting on me. It would also mean they would have to move back into smaller housing. He was so angry that he sold my most prized possession at the flea market: my bicycle. He also threw all my stuff out on the back porch, so he wouldn't have to see me when I came to get it.

I found out my new stepdad Wade was a pothead, but he was also poor so he never had enough pot to keep him mellow. When he didn't have it he was beyond irritable. When I went home with them I found that home was a rickety shell of a trailer with no hot water heater, and no heating system at all. This meant that in order to take daily baths I had to boil large pots of water on the stove top to fill the tub halfway and then fill it the rest of the way with cold water. We ran kerosene heaters for warmth. Wade was a bum, surprise, surprise. He mostly did not work, or would work a couple of weeks before quitting or getting fired. Since my mom had not worked either after giving birth to my sister that meant she was keeping him up on the welfare checks she received on my sister and me. Life was as horrible as I had remembered, but I wanted to be there to watch over and protect my little sister if I could. Who was going to protect me though? I suppose that's why I ended up reaching out to an outside source for some sort of love, support, counsel, I don't really know, but it involved Fred, that man from the convenience store. You remember, the nice man who gave me and my cousin drinks and snacks during our bike-riding days?

Now, the biggest problem with a forty-four-year-old man being "friends" with a fourteen-year-old girl is this: *everything!* In retrospect, I must wonder what the hell were my mother and stepdad thinking by allowing a grown man to come visit me in their home? He would bring me gifts, buy me stuff, and talk to me on the phone about my troubled home life. I suppose because there was no one else to love and no one else to love me I was quite the naive victim, but then fourteen-year-old girls should never be in such a position with an adult male. In a perfect world, a parent would object loudly and go after the old man with a pitchfork, or at least a restraining order, but that is not what happened.

What did happen was I turned fifteen that July and on Christmas Day that same year my mom drove me to Fred's house and left me there to spend the night. That night my most prized, and only pure possession, was taken from me: my virginity. Pain, disgust, confusion, not knowing what to do or how to feel, followed. When my mom picked me up the next morning I told her what had happened. All she had to say was, "Did it hurt? The first time is often painful." Then her next move was to take me to the health department and put me on birth control! To this day, I do not know why she didn't drive me to the hospital for an examination that could have put Fred in jail right then. Due to her lack of concern about it, I thought it must be my fault. Her attitude seemed to imply it's what I should've expected to happen. I wanted out so bad, and when I say out, I meant out of this family, out of this life, out of this world if that were the only option. I was still in high school, 10th grade to be exact, and unable to relate to my peers at all. While they all talked of parties, hanging out and going to football games together, a man old enough to be my father was sexually abusing me!

I wanted a job and I wanted my own money. I needed a new bicycle and I also was going to have to buy my own high school things like annuals, high school ring, etc. My mom had already made that clear. I still had plans to graduate, so when I got a part-time job as a dishwasher on the weekends, I saved and bought my graduation ring two years early. I bought my own annuals and school pictures. I got me that new bicycle, too! When my mom saw all the stuff, she told me I was going to have to start giving her gas money to take me to work and then proposed an amount that would take half my pay. Here's where having your innocence completely lost starts to backfire on such a parent. I told her she could kiss that dream goodbye and that I would just ride my bike to and from work. It was fifteen miles round trip. I didn't mind that part. Riding my bicycle had always been a form of escape for me. A time when my mind could be empty, save for the physical exertion of the ride itself. It was however extremely dangerous because it was always dark when I got off work. I had a flashlight though and I used it like a blinking safety light by waving it over my shoulder when a car would come up behind me. I managed to avoid getting hit by a car that way on the four-lane highway which I had to travel to get home. Mom never offered to rescind her request for gas money, so I kept doing it night after night. Then she told me I was going to have to start paying rent to live at home. My response was, "If I pay you rent, you have no rules or authority over me, or where and when I come and go." I told her. "It doesn't work that way," was her reply. "You still have to live by our rules." I told her she couldn't have her cake and eat it, too. I couldn't believe what she was trying to put on me, to make up for the fact that Wade wasn't working. Wade and I argued a lot. He would stand two inches from my face and scream at me until spit flew. I would taunt him that he could scream in my face till he was blue but that he better know never to touch me again.

Around this time my dad and I had not spoken for several months. He was still being an asshole about me having moved back with my mom. One weekend while my mom, sister and Wade had gone to visit my maternal grandfather I was home alone. I was listening to music, glad to have the tiny trailer to myself when I heard the unmistakable noise of the Gremlin my dad drove at that time. I peeped through a crack in the window shade and sure enough there was Dad's Gremlin turning around in our yard. Then he threw a package out the driver window and sped off. If I haven't made it clear by now that my dad had a penchant for violence, terrorism and general meanness, let this resonate. I waited at least ten minutes to even move. For one, I wanted to make sure that he was indeed gone and not coming back and two, I wanted to give the package time to blow up if it was a bomb. I stepped gingerly onto the porch and out into the yard towards the box. It was white and had black question marks as well as the words Wells Fargo painted on it. I picked it up, gulped, then opened it only to find a rubber hand inside with the fingers positioned to shoot a bird outwards to the opener of the box. Call it posttraumatic stress from childhood but even that scared the shit out of me. So much so that I called Fred to come get me and drive me to my mom where she was two counties over visiting her father. When we got there and I relayed what had happened, Wade was all smug for taking a warrant out on my dad and I guess all I wanted was for my mom to comfort me, or make me feel safe. Instead, they continued their visit while Fred drove me to an out-of-the-way pull-off and sexually violated me again.

Court day came, and being as I was the only witness to see my dad throw out the package, I was called to the stand to testify against my own dad. As if that weren't daunting enough, my dad was no simpleton. The man had done one prison stint, just one. Afterwards he had read law books and studied enough to where he knew way more than the common layman about law. Now he was using that to represent himself, which meant that after the D.A. I would be cross-examined by my own dad. Geez! The sucker pulled out all the punches. The first thing he did was bring out that I had only recently been released from a "mental" hospital. Then he pretty much went on to expose the fact that I had "stabbed" someone in school. He painted me crazy, unstable, violent and unhinged. He walked free. Wow, okay.

Sometime later we moved from that dumpy trailer into a larger, slightly less dumpy trailer. One night, a couple of hours after everyone had gone to sleep, including me, I awoke to the sounds of sobbing from down the hall. I got out of bed and crept down the hall to try and hear better. What was going on, I wondered. My mom was crying, and I heard Wade's voice saying, "You are going to have to put her somewhere; it's either her or me." Then in a whiny burst of tears I heard my mom say, "Well, I can't live without you!" *Okay,* I thought with a sharp stabbing pain to my heart, *that means I'm the one she can live without.* So I packed a small bag, opened my bedroom window and ran away to my nearby cousin's house. I had the cousin take me to my dad's. We had since made peace about what the fuck ever that was with the hand shooting a bird, but he wouldn't let me live with him again either. He said it was too much trouble and hassle to rearrange public housing every time I went back and forth. So, I tried to stay with this cousin of mine. That only lasted a couple of weeks, because she was a married mother of two, and what her husband didn't know was that every night while he worked she would leave those babies with me. She was seeing another guy behind his back and wanted me to keep that secret. I could not, so I tried to eat crow and go back home, but my mother said I couldn't come back.

"What am I supposed to do?" I asked. "I have nowhere to go." "You should have thought about that," she said. Then proceeded to suggest that I get Fred, the old man who had sexually molested me, to get me a place to live. Unfortunately, I did in fact end up on his doorstep asking if perhaps he could help me get my own place and that once in a place I'd pay my own bills. I just couldn't come up with a huge chunk of money to get into a place. This meant getting a different job, because two days a week as a dishwasher would never pay the rent. I got a new job as a cashier and pizza maker that gave me at least five days work each week. I would go to school all day and then work most nights and weekends. I found a small one-bedroom house for rent, and still just fifteen moved into the place all alone. Within a week, my mom came over to tell me that she, Wade and my sister were moving to a town some seventy-five miles away to a property one of her sisters owned that had an empty house on it. They were going to live there rent-free.

As I thought about it more after she left I wondered why I couldn't just go with them. I rode my bicycle to the trailer we had all been living in before she kicked me out. No one was there, so I left her a note telling her that I wanted to go with them. I didn't want to live by myself. I told her I loved her and my sister and would try harder to get along with Wade. It was all for naught though because when I came home from work that night she had left a response note on my door. Unlike mine to her that had been on notebook paper, hers to me was on what looked like a hastily torn piece of brown paper bag. Fred had given me a ride that night so that I wouldn't have to ride my bike home in the dark. As we stepped onto the stoop to go inside I found the note stuck in the crack of the screen door. I still have that note to this day. Never really knew why I kept it.

The Brown Paper Bag Letter

Jvonne,
We came by to tell you our plans changed. We will probably be leaving before the weekend. I don't know if I'll see you before I leave or not. We may go to our new place tomorrow. If I don't see you before I'll try to see you on the 6th of May. I found your note. Don't give mama the sad I don't want you to leave. You have your own life, be happy and make the best you can of it. I love you no matter where I am and I will write to you. I'll also get an address where you can write me. I am still around. I am still alive. Just in another town.
Love Mama

CHAPTER 5

Complete Loss of Innocence

I REMEMBER FRED SITTING DOWN in a chair in the front room, with an expression of disbelief. "They've abandoned you," he said, "and left the responsibility of you on me." This made me cry, because it sounded like everybody wanted rid of me, and I crawled up on his lap like a child, and cried. He did not comfort me like a father, or a parent, or even a friend; instead he had sex with me.

I couldn't make enough money at my lousy part-time job to ever fully pay my rent and utilities. This meant that every month Fred had to cover the difference, which by words unspoken meant I would continue to be sexually molested. I can't tell you what really goes through the mind at times like those, because really you just blank out to keep from being sick. I felt dirty. I felt disgusting. I felt violated in every way. Feelings of disgust and shame became my everyday.

It was summer and I was still having to ride my bicycle everywhere. I was having to go all summer to school if I wanted to be promoted to 11th grade. I had failed 10th grade only by excessive absences and tardiness. No one knew what was going on "at home." I covered it. No one knew that my father lived twenty-eight miles away in the next county and that I hardly ever saw him. No one knew that my mother had abandoned me and moved some seventy-five miles away to a farther part of the state. No one knew that after school, I'd ride that same bike another ten miles to get to my job at the pizza place, and work all night. That after work I'd ride another eight miles home on that bike, to this small house where a forty-five-year-old man would be waiting for sex. Even the bike riding itself was becoming dangerous.

One afternoon on my way home from my job, I was cutting around the local park as I always did. There was a small car with four people tucked in it, parked at the park, facing the road. Three were black and one was white—all adults. I noticed only because one of them yelled something derogatory out the window: "Hey, you white bitch! White bitch! I dare you to say something!" I really did contemplate ignoring it completely and just pedaling faster and hoping they wouldn't follow me. Then I also realized that if I acted scared they would come after me. Who were they anyway? Just assholes getting their kicks, or could they be harboring ill intentions? I'm in the curve turning when they yell out again, "White bitch, too scared to say anything!" *Ah, here we go left eye*, I thought, *hang in there!* Then even as my legs began to pedal stronger and faster, I yelled out in response as I flipped them the bird, "Y'all fuckers can go to hell!" They immediately started their car and came after me. I do remember pedaling that fucking bike harder and faster than I'd ever pedaled it in my life, because I felt my life depended on it. I rode that bike so hard that somehow I had enough of a lead that I was able to come over the hump of the road on which I lived and see clearly that the Baptist church was having some sort of outside function. I coasted into that church parking lot like a bat out of hell on that bicycle, with the car of would-be assailants hot on my trail. However, when I pulled up to the steps of that church and got off my bike and stood with the group, my haters made 'bang bang' gestures with their fingers out the window, but they had to ride on by unless they wanted to kill a revival full of people. So, I waved, like the smartass that I was, and watched them go up and down the road in front of the church several times before finally giving up. Then I ate a couple of Jesus's free hot dogs at the preacher's insistence and went home, which was just across the street and down two houses.

A few months into this atrocious arrangement, I tried to get a better-paying job. I switched to waiting tables. It was often midnight when I would get home. Getting up and going to school every morning became next to impossible. I had made it to 11th grade by the hair of my chin and knew I needed to buckle down on my studies. However, I was physically exhausted and mentally traumatized by the life I was having to live. In an effort to break free of some of it I found a boardinghouse that would rent me a room that I could pay for easily myself, and get away from the constant abuse I was accepting in return for mere survival and basic needs. Despite the move, I could not improve my attendance at school. I was late almost every day, sometimes by half the day.

The principle was a nice man who seemed to sympathize with my struggle. He suggested that I let Vocational Rehabilitation get involved. They had a program that I could do that was a half-day work/half-day school deal. I was willing to give anything a try at this point to stay in school. However, my emotional stability was fading fast. It was as if I could feel the cracks in the foundation of my soul. I was fast becoming irritable and cynical about most everything.

Soon sixteen, I was now a sexual being whether I wanted to be one or not, which for the record, I didn't! Like most little girls, I had once held dreams of being someone's virginal bride and spending life together with my one true love. Now, I just didn't want rape to be the only sexual experience I had! It happened that I would soon meet a boy around my age at the vocational rehabilitation center the school had sent me to. His name was Ron. He was no bigger than me in stature, black hair, cute, wearing a leather jacket and dating a girl I knew from school. Ron was there because he had a very mild case of cerebral palsy that caused a slight limp when he walked, and he needed a job skill. He was eighteen and already out of school. I caught him looking at me and he would smile. I would smile and kind of shake my head thinking how silly of me, of course he didn't want me. I was tainted and somehow he would see that. Plus he already had a girlfriend, right? Well, they broke up quickly for some reason and he began talking to me soon after, and gave me his number.

Around this same time, Wade had dumped my mom and brought her back to town. Apparently, he had started telling her that she was old, ugly and fat, and just left her. Due to that grand fact, she had invited me to move back in with her and my sister to the projects, where welfare would provide her free housing. I really didn't trust her but I wanted so badly to get that high school diploma and be the first in this dysfunctional family to have one that I gave up my boardinghouse room and moved back home. I just wanted to focus on this Vocational Rehabilitation program and finish school.

I needed a car of my own because I was stuck driving Fred's car. I felt trapped in that regard since I had no money. One day Fred took me to a used car lot to test drive something. While he and I drove this potential purchase, we pulled over to look under the hood and do the usual pre-purchase check. I had cut the car off and now it wouldn't start for some reason. That sucked because we were about a mile into the local entrance to the national forest and the nearest phone or store was a mile's walk away. This was pre- cell phones! We agreed that I would stay locked up in the car and he would walk to the phone to call the car dealer.

While I was sitting there another car pulled in behind me and a man got out and walked up to the driver's side where I sat. I had the window partially down for air and he asked me if I needed help. I told him someone had already gone for help but thanks anyway. He looked oddly from side to side; his expression was creepy and he asked me if I was sure I didn't need any help, to which I again politely declined. He stood there still and I was feeling strange vibes when he reached through the open window and grabbed my left breast as he said, "Wooooo!" I was paralyzed with fear. I remember thinking, *Oh my God, I've already been violated by someone I know. Now a stranger is probably going to rape and kill me right here in the national forest!* Thank God, he just laughed and casually walked back to his car and drove away. I don't think I took a breath until he had pulled away and went in the opposite direction.

Once he was gone I got out of the disabled test drive and ran to the road screaming and waving my arms to flag down the next car. Just as a harmless-looking old man stopped to see what was wrong with me Fred showed back up with help, so I ran to him instead. I was crying, breathless and anxiety riddled, trying to tell him what had happened. As the help he had brought was jump-starting the test drive, I described the stranger who had attacked me. Fred had seen the guy pass by and recognized him as a customer from the store where he worked. He even knew his name. As we drove back to the car lot I told Fred I was going to the police to have this breast-grabbing guy charged with sexual assault. This seemed to make Fred angry, probably because he was guilty of so much more. He began to insult and further degrade me by saying if I didn't dress like such a little whore maybe these things wouldn't keep happening to me.

I will always believe that was the day I snapped completely and the light went out for a very long and painful time. I screamed at him, hit him and called him filthy names. Then I got out of the test drive, got into his car and left him standing there in that car lot. As I peeled out of the parking lot like a bat out of Hell I cried over the derogatory comments he had made. Cried over my lost virginity. Cried over the stranger's assault, but mostly cried because of such feelings of violation. I no longer loved myself, nay,

I didn't even like me. My self-respect was gone. I felt like a prostitute of sorts in that I had been sexually assaulted for so long that abnormal was my normal. I had never felt so angry in my life, as I drove that piece-of-shit car up to ninety miles an hour and threw it in reverse. I loved the way the gears ground. It sounded like the transmission might fall out. I pulled over and parked, got out my knife and slit the front and back seats to shit then I poured motor oil all over the backseat, then I got back in and ran it into some things!

Through hot, angry tears I drove it straight to that boy Ron's new job and asked him if he would kindly follow me to the convenience store where Fred worked because I would be needing a ride. Without question Ron followed as I sputtered Fred's car into the parking lot. I walked in, opened the ice cream freezer that stood in front of the register and threw Fred's key deep down into it where he would have to take everything out to get to it. Then I walked out, got into the car with Ron and he took me to the police department. I did file charges against the stranger for the unprovoked assault. Turns out the weird-ass stranger had a criminal record already for such behavior against women, but even as a prior offender he only got two years probation, no jail time.

About a month later, my dad finally found out about Fred's ongoing sexual abuse of me and was able as my parent to file charges of rape against him. I was an emotional mess, as day by day I would swing back and forth between wanting Fred prosecuted and having some sick sense of loyalty to him for having taken care of me. I suppose you could liken it to a mild case of Stockholm syndrome. In the end he only got thirty days in jail, followed by two years probation, with mandatory counseling. Afterwards I came to feel very angry about that, thinking how he had taken something from me that I could never get back, and all it was worth to the judicial system was thirty days? Let's just say I was damaged beyond repair. My faith in the judicial system was ruined. And God? As far as I was concerned, He had forsaken me completely.

Rage

It seeps into my brain, into my heart, into my soul
To destroy and wreak havoc, destruction its only goal
Stronger than an army, crazy as a lunatic
It takes control of my emotions, and makes my body sick
It drives me past the limit, of ever understanding
Picks me up, flies me high, then gives me a crash landing
It comes from fear and sadness, it's filled with so much
hate
Eats me from the inside, always trying to propagate
The madness and the illness, looking for compensation
Trying to seek revenge, for my current situation
I am its host and prisoner, my body is the cage
I'm way past any anger, this friend of mine is rage

CHAPTER 6

Hell Hath No Fury Like a Damaged Teenaged Girl

So where was God in all this? The Real God, the one I mentioned at the beginning of this book? Well, that was my question and believe me when I say I did not ask nicely. I was starting to think He was a real asshole, but we'll come back to that.

The scariest part of all to follow is that I was *never* on drugs. I *never* drank alcohol. Hell, I *never* even had a cigarette cross my lips. Mostly because I did not like feeling out of control and therefore feared drugs. I certainly wanted nothing to do with alcohol as in my mind it had ruined my parents' marriage, amongst other things. Despite being clean, at this point I was mentally and emotionally unstable and hell-bent on sharing my pain with others. It didn't help my sanity or my love for God much when my mom's husband Wade started coming back around trying to win her back. I suppose Mom wasn't "old, ugly, or fat" enough to keep him from coming around once he was jobless again.

I had started dating Ron and shortly after, having sex with him. Mostly because I needed an experience other than rape. My mom would let him come over, go into my bedroom with me, stay the night even. In fact, she was starting to be gone on weekends to be with Wade. Ron was allowed to stay with me all weekend while she was gone. One weekend while Ron and I were out and about in his car someone rear-ended us and there was no headrest behind me. I suffered a horrible whiplash to the neck and it honestly hurt so bad I thought it was broken. Paramedics strapped me down to a hard board gurney and put a clamp around my neck so I wouldn't move my head. X-rays showed a major shift and misalignment of vertebrae in my neck, so they put me in a neck brace and told me not to lift anything or move unnecessarily for six weeks. I went to physical therapy and a chiropractor for treatment. I was just three weeks in and still in a neck brace when my mother announced that she was moving back in with Wade. He was sitting beside her on the couch when she made this announcement.

"Okay, what am I supposed to do?" I asked. "Well, I guess you'll have to find somewhere else to live," said my mom. "So, you're kicking me out again?" I asked incredulously. "Oh, you'll have thirty days," she said, like it was some sort of blessing. "You know, you are really some piece of work, not to mention extremely stupid," I said. To which Wade jumped up and approached me way too close for comfort, yelling that I would not talk to my mother that way. *Oh, here we go again!* I thought.

I informed Wade that unlike the last time he had gotten in my face, I wouldn't bother to call my dad should he put his hands on me again. I had a knife sheathed to my side at all times now and I patted it for effect. I wanted him to know that I wouldn't mind sticking it in him should he feel the need to touch me! I think he bought that I would stab him, maybe because of my earlier school incident with a knife, because he shrank back a little. I'd be lying if I said I didn't enjoy the power that anger seemed to bring and I enjoyed it even more if it brought fear and panic to the other party. As far as I was concerned anger beat the hell out of despair!

Never one to support me in situations like this, my mom started yelling for me to get out right then. So, I called Ron to come get me and my stuff, but when he got there she wouldn't let him come in to carry my things out, even though I wasn't supposed to lift or move anything unnecessarily. I told her she would have to carry it out then, which she refused to do. Instead, she and Wade both sat on the couch and watched me struggle with boxes from my room down the hall to the front doorway, in a neck brace may I remind you. Ron would then lean in the doorframe to get the box and carry it for me the rest of the way to the car. He commented on how shitty a thing it was that they were doing to me. When he did, Wade lunged at him and told him to get off the porch, even the walkway, and was advancing on him so strongly that Ron lost his balance and fell (remember he had a slight case of cerebral palsy).

I abandoned my box-getting and ran ahead to Ron's car. I jumped in and grabbed Ron's pellet pistol which was solid black and looked real. I tapped on the window with it so Wade would see it. When he did, the fear in his eyes as he ran away from Ron and back into the apartment was priceless. As Ron got in the car, all shaken up by a grown man accosting him like that, I told him we would come back to get the rest of my stuff some other time when they were gone. We had to sleep in the car that night. The next day, after surveying the scene and ascertaining that no one was home, I used my key to get in and we started getting the remainder of my stuff. I'd pack, Ron would carry. He had gone outside with a box and seemed to be taking forever, so I went out to see what was taking so long. A cop had him bent over the trunk of his car and was putting handcuffs on him.

"Wait, what are you doing?" I asked the cop. "Are you Jvonne Hubbard?" the cop asked, rather than answer me. "Yes, I live here, what is this?" I asked again. "You are under arrest as well," he told me as he reached for another set of handcuffs. Ron and I were arrested, both charged with warrants claiming that we had both pointed guns at Wade and my mom! She had signed a warrant to that effect even though she had never even been outside when it happened, or a part of what went on out there! So, my mom had me put in a jail cell for the first time in my life and she lied to do it. Congratulations Mom, I now also hate you.

Let me take the time to point out here that this entire police force hated my dad. They knew and loathed his ability to get away with so much. He had never been sent away (save once) for anything he did because they never had proof. You'll remember from my childhood, however, that he was quite the criminal. Unfortunately for the police, despite his ignorant choices he knew the law well enough to represent himself often and walk away free. Those same police remembered my mom as their former janitor. A "poor lady" done wrong by my dad. As for me, I guess they figured the apple didn't fall too far from the tree. So, here I was being judged for my father's reputation. Angrier and more dysfunctional than to begin with, this is how I figured it: *So they think I'm a criminal, aye? Well, let me show them criminal for real,* I thought. So, it began that I stopped giving a fuck about most everything for a good two-year stint.

Ron had been living in a single room at the same boarding-house I had once lived in. He had gotten it to be closer to me, in fact, but now that I had nowhere to go he gave it up to be homeless with me. We slept in his car for a few nights before I sucked it up enough to go to my dad and ask him if we could live in his camper while we tried to find a home. My stepmother had recently given birth to a son and they had bought their own mobile home. In addition he had acquired a small pull-behind camper that stayed parked alongside his trailer. Ron and I lived like that for several weeks. During that time local social services and a nice preacher man combined their efforts to find and put me in one of those low-income housing apartments of my own. The way they figured it, since my mother had abandoned me I was the one in need of housing. Even though I was still underage they opted not to put me in a group home, citing that I would only disrupt it most likely. I have to admit, they weren't wrong. I had no intention of ever being under anyone's control ever again, parents included. Ron needed shelter too and so we lived together in the welfare apartment that I was provided by the state. For the next two years this boy would put up with and find himself involved in quite the emotional roller coaster ride.

That spastic bladder problem of mine that had started in 6th grade had reared its ugly head again and was growing increasingly chronic. The discomfort was at times continuous and relentless. Now that I had been raped however, I associated any and all discomfort of the lower body with violation. When this would happen, I would fly into an otherwise unprovoked rage and literally tear, rip, punch or throw anybody or anything that chanced to stop me. Often this was Ron trying to comfort me, or hold me, but I didn't want to be touched in those moments and so I would lash out at him.

Holidays would come and my mother never bothered to contact me. That would send me into some sort of mental spaz that I couldn't control at the time and I'd go off, punching, kicking, screaming, and cussing whoever or whatever was around. Then one day during one of those tirades the Bible hit the floor and it struck me that all of this was God's fault! After all, He had allowed all this to happen. He had done nothing to stop it. I had once thought He loved me as much as I loved Him but in that moment of feeling completely forsaken, I figured He could kiss my ass, too! While in that mental state I poured cooking oil all over the Bible and yelled at the top of my lungs, "That's what I think of your Word!"

I spent weekends flattening car tires and busting out headlights on cars parked at churches. Saturdays for Seventh Day Adventist and other Christians on Sundays. I remember wondering if they could keep their faith while when they were at church such senselessness could attack them. Why didn't their God protect their precious, expensive cars? I guess I wanted to punish anyone who would trust God. I continued to talk to God only to make sure He understood how much I hated Him! Then I would fall into a heap on the apartment floor and cry until the snot ran in puddles. By now Ron was almost afraid to try and intervene anymore, because I would only hit, scratch, claw or bite him if he touched me.

When it came to displaying all my hate and rage however, I was an equal opportunity offender. I didn't leave "sinners" off the list. During this same period of time we happened upon a den of whores. Just to clarify, prostitutes standing on the corners of this one block of downtown Asheville NC. I was both shocked and disgusted. In my mind it was beyond comprehension that women were standing out there with the risk of disease and defilement by choice. Sex was a very touchy subject with me. I had had my purity ruined, and these women were freely ruining theirs again and again and again. So, I did the only thing that my severely warped, emotionally unhinged mind could come up with. I shot them with that same pellet pistol I had once pointed at my stepfather Wade. Ron would drive and I would pop the prostitutes out the passenger window. Not once, twice, or even three times, I mean we made a weekend ritual out of that shit. Until one weekend the ladies had a "slickster"-looking, suit-wearing, cane-toting pimp with them and as we drove by I swear that motherfucker pulled his cane apart! I told Ron to gas it because I wasn't entirely sure that shit wouldn't disassemble into a gun! We shut down that little weekend game after that experience.

Ron and I often had nothing to eat for days; even though he worked it was barely enough to keep the lights and water on in the apartment. There were days we just sucked ketchup packets we were so hungry. Let me tell you, hunger did nothing to quell the angry beast that lay constantly beneath the surface of my psyche. Once, in a tirade over hunger alone, I covered the entire living room floor with cornmeal and flour. I was so angry that such things were in the house with no way to make them into anything to actually eat. Every now and then, but never enough for it to look like a habit, we would go to a local drive-thru at their busiest hour and claim to have had a large fries left off our order. Or perhaps an apple pie, a taco, something small enough that it wouldn't be contested or argued over by the window staff.

We were poverty stricken, anxiety riddled and so desperate that Ron turned to stealing money from an old man that had held affection for him in his childhood. It is disgusting to think back on, but when you're down to sucking ketchup packets for a meal and have no tools or support from which to draw upon, bad decisions run rampant! After four visits that cost this man over two hundred dollars, he shut the door in our faces on that fifth knock at his door. This led to further desperation and misplaced anger on my part, which led us back to his house in the middle of the night to spray paint profanity all over the outside of it. A short time later we were both arrested and charged with vandalism and larceny. On our first court appearance I had instructed Ron the way my dad always instructed me about crime and subsequent legal troubles: Plead not guilty. Make them give you a court-appointed attorney, wear down the system with continuances, and eventually, 80 percent of the time they will throw it out. However, once on the stand Ron crumbled under questioning and pleaded guilty. This angered me royally because if he pleaded guilty as the main culprit, how could I as an accessory plead not guilty? I had my court hearing put off and then as we were exiting the courthouse and re-entering our car, I began to threaten Ron verbally. I told him that when we got to my dad's trailer, which was just a few miles from the courthouse, he better jump out and start running because I was going to beat his ass! I don't know why it shocked me once we got there that Ron did just that!

I didn't even have the gear in Park before he had opened his door and jumped out. Running as best he could with a limp, out of the trailer park towards the main road. This infuriated me, and I ran after him. While trying to grab ahold of his leather jacket several of my fingernails got torn off, which incensed me further. Without missing a beat, since I had the car keys in my hand and on the key ring was a mini-size tear gas, I sprayed him in both eyes to try and slow him down enough to catch. By this point my dad had heard the ruckus and was running after me, running after Ron. He was wiping his eyes furiously while still running, I was trying to shove him out into oncoming traffic, and my big, burly, mean-looking dad was behind me screaming, "Jvonne stop, you're going to kill him!" I don't even remember how all that ended, that's how lost in my own internal rage I could get during that period of my life. I do know Ron didn't die and we both ended up sitting in my dad's living room and later going on home without further incident.

Despite all this, in my normal moments I still had a heart for anyone else suffering and often got myself into situations of trying to help someone when I couldn't even help myself. So, when Ron and I found a grown man in a neck brace sleeping under the outside stairwell of the public housing apartment complex we lived in, I was drawn like a magnet to his plight. He had been living with his girlfriend a couple doors down but she had beaten the shit out of him and put him out. In time, I would come to understand why, but for then we felt sorry for him. We told him he could stay a couple nights with us. He worked as a butcher at a local grocery store and so he brought steak, hamburger and chicken home almost every night. Based on food alone those couple of nights turned into weeks. However, as the weeks went on he really started to grate my already raw nerves. He would walk into the bathroom even if you were in the shower and just use the toilet. He would enter our room without knocking and sit on our bed and talk, never respecting personal space. Apart from the moderate food he supplied he didn't contribute anything towards actual living expenses. I was reaching a breaking point already when one of those urination/bladder spasm episodes started on the 4th of July, which led to an emotional outburst on my part. This led to Ron begging me to take the meds a doctor had recently prescribed me for anxiety and depression. So, I did and that led to me falling asleep.

Apparently, while I was asleep my cousin Kaylee had shown up with her boyfriend to see if we wanted to ride over the state line to get some fireworks. Ron made the executive decision that

I needed to stay asleep and rest, so he and our houseguest went with them. Now, as to why he left no note I can only guess he figured they would be back before I ever woke up, but he was wrong. When I woke up and went through the apartment to find it empty I started to panic. *Oh my God, he's left me; like everybody else, he's abandoned me!* Then I went to the bathroom and experienced that pain again and went into the anger with no one around. I grabbed my knife, went outside and paced back and forth in front of the apartments. Ron's car was still there so I figured our houseguest had taken him off somewhere on foot and I was livid. I'm sure to anyone watching out their window I looked insane, mumbling to myself about what I was going to do to Ron for leaving me.

Pacing like a wild animal in front of his car, I had a knife sheathed to my side. Then I saw my cousin's car coming. She was waving out the window; her boyfriend was driving. When they pulled up, Ron and our houseguest got out of the back seat. Ron was smiling. I suppose he thought I'd be happy they had fireworks, but no one got to explain that before I had accosted him with a serious slap across the face that challenged his balance. Everyone gasped as I pulled that knife out and started waving it around like a maniac at Ron, as I cussed, accused, and threatened. Now to this point, our houseguest had never seen this level of breakdown out of me. I suppose he was frightened for Ron's safety, but he made the mistake of taking the attention off Ron and onto himself. He stood between us and asked me not to hurt Ron. All that did was give the bull a different red flag to zone in on. I advanced on him then, shaking the knife in his face, telling him all the pent-up things I'd wanted to say about how aggravating I found his presence to be, how he was to blame for the whole thing and how if he didn't get the fuck out of there right then, I would stab him! With that he ran as fast as he could down the street, away. His fear brought me temporary satisfaction, enough to abandon any further thought of harming Rick. My cousin Kaylee risked putting her arms around me and hugged me. She calmed me the rest of the way down, and we ended up having a pretty good evening given the circumstances!

The next day there came a sharp rap on the apartment door. From previous encounters I recognized the knock as police. Before I opened the door I put in my NWA cassette tape, so the song "Fuck The Police" would blare the chorus behind me as I opened the door. There to arrest me for assault was a detective. I guess I hadn't considered it much, because I hadn't actually assaulted anyone except Ron, but you can't just threaten people verbally while brandishing a knife, which, had I been altogether sane, I would have realized. Also probably wouldn't have fueled the fire with such disrespectful music if rational had been a part of my thought process, but at that time sadly it was not.

Fortunately for me, the county had a mediation program where cases that were considered minor were sent to see if they could be resolved without prosecution. It was at this mediation program that I met the most wonderful lady I had ever known. The mediator was an older lady of about sixty-five, who was a court liaison for the program. Her name was Miriam, and her job was to listen to both sides of the story, and try to cultivate a peaceful resolution that both parties could agree upon. My former houseguest got to go first, as he was technically the victim, however when it was my turn to speak I told everything about how we had tried to help him, and why my behavior had gone all extreme. Still to this day I have no idea how that lady saw in just an hour that there might be more to me than just a dysfunctional teenager moving toward total self-destruction, but she called me aside after the meeting and told me she would like to help me if she could. She insisted on giving me fifty dollars a month, which if we conserved like crazy could help feed us every month. I wish I had been in a position to fully appreciate what she was trying to do, but I'm sad to say I was not at that time. Her act of kindness was out of balance with just how fucked up every other aspect of my day-to-day reality was, so life continued to become more dysfunctional.

Bad Apple

Cut from the same cloth, bad apple from the same tree
I know all the assumptions, but y'all don't know me
I've lived through his violence, I've seen all his crime
Of course, I act like him, my anger now in its prime
What choice has life left me, what tools shall I grab
All I know is to lash out, protect myself, stab
He's imperfect and evil, by darkness he reigns
I'm just trying to emulate him, to stave off the pain

CHAPTER 7

Partners in Crime

IT WAS THE EARLY '90S and my dad had started showing signs of being back full in with the KKK. I knew because weird shit started happening. Like, once while Ron and I were over at my dad's trailer a black Lincoln Continental limo pulled up. Out stepped a man sharply dressed. He had on dark gray slacks with matching sports coat, complete with gold chain. He looked like a mobster, at least the way they portray them in the movies. The man came in, sat down, chatted with my dad, then stood up for my step-mom to take pictures of he and my dad shaking hands with the rebel flag on display behind them. When he left, I had to ask, "Who was that?" My dad told me it was James Earl Ray's brother!

Then sometime later that same year, there was one hell of a ruckus that broke out in my dad's trailer park between a white woman and her Hispanic boyfriend. I'm not certain what, if any, relationship this woman had with my dad prior to that day, but on that day she marched over to my dad's trailer mid-argument with her boyfriend and asked if she could borrow one of his guns. The way my dad told it later, he asked her why and she told him she was going to shoot her son-of-a-bitch boyfriend. Citing in his mind how much disdain he held for interracial romances, he gleefully and gladly handed her one out of his gun cabinet. Then she did in fact go back out into the open courtyard of the trailer park and blast her boyfriend's chest out. The murder made the front page of the local newspaper and my dad's gun was confiscated as evidence. I have no idea how he didn't get into legal trouble or go to prison himself for that type of involvement in something so heinous, but he didn't.

Also, if you're old enough to remember the standoff on Ruby Ridge in northern Idaho, circa 1992, then it will be noteworthy to tell how my dad sold his trailer home to try and get there to help Randy Weaver. Yes, never one to consider his family first, my dad sold his mobile home for just $2,000. Packed my stepmother, stepbrother and less-than-two-year-old brother in the car and headed to Idaho with guns a-blazing! Apparently, Mr. Weaver was rumored to have Aryan Nation ties and that was what inspired my dad. He was halfway there when U.S. Marshals and FBI agents killed Mr. Weaver's wife, son and family dog, which ended the siege. All for nothing, my dad had to come back to no home and just rent a dumpy trailer to throw his family back into.

A short time later he established ties with Charles Manson through the mail. Everyone knows Manson for cold-blooded murders, but might not remember that they were committed for the purpose of hopefully starting a race war. This was the part that appealed to my dad, I'm sure. I remember not believing him at first, even when he showed me the letters signed by Manson, but then I also saw my dad sell those letters to some professional-looking dude at the flea market. To hear my dad tell it, the professional-looking man was a writer and paid top dollar for authenticated letters from serial killers. If that had been the only reason my dad drummed up a relationship with Charles Manson it would have been bad enough, but he also accepted collect calls from Manson. In fact, so desperate for me to not keep thinking it was bullshit he had me answer his phone on one such occasion as he was waiting for said call. I picked it up at my dad's request and sure enough an automated voice said: "You have a collect call from the California State Prison from: (and then in his own creepy voice which that automated system allowed him to say for himself I heard) "Charles Manson". Okay. I handed the phone to my dad. He wanted me to stay on and talk to this freak but I declined. Seems Manson had started to believe my dad was some reincarnation of his favorite uncle, or something crazy like that and would call him Uncle Joe! For his part, my dad kept a picture of Manson in a frame that he displayed on a shelf in his home. He also bragged that his association with Manson had landed him on an FBI watch list. Years later my sister related to me that my dad had her talk to Charles Manson once on the phone too and he had spoken to her. "Hello, little girl," he had said.

By mid-1992 I had run into an old play pal, a girl who had lived in the neighborhood I had lived in around age twelve. We recognized each other and started to chat. Her home life sounded unpleasant, plus I had disregard for parents and authority in general, so I invited her to live with Ron and me. She began to copy my style of dress: all black, leather jacket, black nail polish and red lips. She even bleached her hair to my shade of blonde. I wish I could have seen it for the creepiness it was, instead of taking it as a compliment. I guess I got the "Single White Female" treatment before I even knew what that was!

My girlfriend was younger than me by two years. I had finally hit eighteen by now and she was sixteen and still trying to go to school. She would come home sometimes depressed or scared over how people were treating her at school. It sounded familiar to me—persecution for how you dress or look—but she couldn't stand up to any of them; she was very dainty in stature physically and had zero backbone for fending them off. As fate in a fucked-up world would have it though, she, Ron and I went walking around town one Sunday afternoon, just to alleviate boredom and get some physical exercise. It sure beat sitting around the apartment contemplating the dead-end horror that seemed to be our lives! Suddenly a car horn honked; it startled all of us, and we looked to the road to see a convertible with three people in it go by. As it did a rather large girl in the backseat screamed, "*Whore!*" The car sped off with the three occupants laughing. "Who the fuck was that?" I asked out loud. My poor friend's eyes were wide with fear as she told me it was one of the main girls who bullied her at school. I breathed hard and heavy for first-hand experience with that plight, but we continued walking.

Then the car came back by again. They had turned around just to pass by us and yell some more. "Slut!" the girl yelled. So, I yelled back, "Go fuck yourself!" and flipped them all off. Ron and my friend urged that we just hurry home, but I was like, "To hell with that; we have every right to walk down the street without being afraid." I just kept the normal pace. The car came back, zipped in front of us at a pedestrian crossing and parked up on the sidewalk in front of a fire hydrant, right at the corner of an open drugstore. All three got out and approached us, but only the big girl from the backseat walked up into our personal space, and stood right in front of my friend. She towered over her and looked menacing as she asked, "What did you say?" To which I leaned over to be the face she was looking at and said, "She didn't say shit, but I said go fuck yourself!" The bully looked taken aback. "What?" she exclaimed, like she couldn't believe anyone would repeat themselves in her domineering presence. I'll admit I was just as scared on the inside as anyone there. For one, there was still that eye that didn't need to be punched out again, not to mention how I didn't need any more trouble, but what are you going to do, right?

"What exactly is your problem?" I asked her. "We haven't done one thing to you, yet you yell out these obscene, derogatory comments; you don't know us." Her reply: "I don't like the way she dresses, or you for that matter. You both look like whores." My reply: "Yeah well, I don't necessarily care for how you dress either. It's rather boring and does nothing to hide the fact that you're a fat-ass cow." I knew this would end all talk, and so almost instinctively at this point, my right hand was already on the sheath of my trusty little friend, dagger. I saw her eyes change. I only had a split second to consider my prospects, which were slim in my opinion. She outweighed me, out sized me and I had that damn eye to consider. When she drew back her fist, my last thought was, *Here we go again!* I always carried that dagger on my side. I felt way too vulnerable without it, given my undesirable lifestyle. I yanked it from its sheath and collided with her arm mid-punch. Only this time, I had no plans to run from the repercussions, just to own whatever happened. Upon collision, as she ripped the lace glove from my free arm, I did run into the drugstore, still with knife in hand just to be the one to call the police. I asked the older lady behind the cash register to call the police for me. Before she could even ascertain what was going on, to my shock and surprise the girl came in after me and chased me around a counter or two until suddenly she realized her arm was cut and bleeding. Then she shrieked and ran back outside. I sat down in the middle of the floor. My friend and Ron came in and sat with me. I said, "Well fellas, the cops are coming; you know I'm going to go to jail."

We waited and they did come. I was horrified to find out that one of the attending police officers was the cut girl's uncle and that it was his very own daughter who had been driving the car they had been in. I was terrified! I figured given the circumstances I would be going up the river for attempted murder. They handcuffed me and confiscated my knife. They even confiscated my friend's knife too, because like everything else she had bought herself one just like mine. They put me in the back of a police cruiser and took me to the jail to stand before the magistrate. Luckily on that day, the one magistrate that was not biased against me over who my father was, listened to my account and the cut girl's, my witnesses, her witnesses, and then determined fairly thus: If you park on the sidewalk in front of a fire hydrant and approach someone threateningly and call them foul names, and in the process get stabbed, you pretty much brought that shit on yourself!

We were both charged with "simple affray," which means fighting in public to the terror of said public (like the poor woman in the drugstore who had to call the police). Eventually, that girl and I ended up at that same mediation center where I had first met Miriam. Although that day it was a different mediator, which I was glad of because I was quite the asshole once it was my turn to talk. However, because the cut girl was considered the victim she spoke first. The girl who had been so mean and threatening on the sidewalk now sat there trying to look demure in her "normal" looking clothes, talking sweetly about how she just wanted me to pay her hospital bill, that she didn't want this to go to court. She didn't want a criminal record because she was going to college after high school and needed a clear record. I sat there listening to this and feeling really pissy on the inside, so once it was my turn to talk I said, "Well, here's the thing: I dropped out of school my junior year, got my GED, and never had the faintest opportunity to go to college. Also, I have a criminal record a mile long already, and don't really give a shit if it gets a little bit longer on your account. I'm poverty stricken, so I have no money, therefore I won't be paying your little hospital bill that you brought upon yourself when you stepped out of your car and got in my face!"

She and the mediator just sat there, mouths gaping, but in the end she had to accept defeat, pay her own bill and let bygones be bygones if she really wanted to continue life with a clean and spotless record.

Miriam continued to take me out to lunch about once a month, to talk, to see how I was doing and the like. After this latest episode, even though she agreed it was not my fault necessarily, she suggested perhaps there were a few things I could do to lessen the likelihood of such episodes. "Like what?" I asked. "Well, like maybe not wearing that," she said, as she pointed to my blackened nails and leather jacket. "You could maybe wear softer colors, tone the shade of your lipstick down," she continued. I knew she meant well and later in life I would even see the validity, but at that moment in time it sounded to me like she and the world thought somehow I should conform to blend in and not rock the boat. My opinion was, if how I dressed was all it took to rock someone's boat, then it was their problem, not mine! Miriam asked me to come live with her and her husband and let her send me to college. It was a grand offer, but my question was, "What about Ron?" Trying to be sensitive and put it like a lady she told me I was an adult and could still date Ron in my off time. It warmed my heart that this lady seemed to care for me and what was going to happen to me, but I wasn't going to leave Ron homeless. My loyalty, however distorted or misplaced, for whatever it was worth, was with him. Plus, I knew my fucked-up nature enough to know that I couldn't live up to her well-intentioned expectations, and so I declined.

My girlfriend, whom I had now stabbed someone for, continued to live with us but she continued to spiral deeper into her own emotional dysfunction. I'm sure we were not good for each other at that time, but of course there we were. Ron had gotten a better-paying nighttime job at a factory nearby. At night when he was working she and I were alone in our boredom and teenaged insanity. On one such evening I suggested we make prank phone calls to amuse ourselves, and the sort I was making were rather childish things like: "Hey is your refrigerator running . . . pause . . . well you better go catch it!" or "Do you have Prince Albert in the can . . . pause . . . well you better let him out." Then it was her turn and she used the phonebook to find churches. Apparently, she was on the outs with God above and beyond the level that I was! She took it to the next level, calling up preachers and saying things about Jesus Christ that I can't even for the sake of telling my story repeat. Then she would make odd remarks about wanting to put pins in their eyes to hold them still and make them watch her defecate on the Bible. My reaction was twofold: shock that she had that in her, and nervous laughter because it was such crazy-sounding stuff!

Ron and I started to wonder if she was mentally ill, which says a lot considering my own emotional state at the time. Then we had a personal incident happen that we couldn't readily explain. A rifle that Ron kept in the apartment went missing. There was no sign of forced entry, which left us to suspect that for some reason my friend had just handed it out the door to someone. We didn't confront her about it though. Instead, Ron just went to the police department to fill out a complaint so they would investigate. I'm sure they didn't bother, because I think they figured we were the last people on the planet who needed a gun. Even I would have to agree there, given my penchant for losing my mind now and again.

Within a couple of days however, cops came to the apartment and arrested my girlfriend. Ron and I figured they had somehow concluded she had stolen the gun. So, we followed them down to the station to see what was up. They kept her back there for a long time before coming out to say she was under arrest, but that was not the surprise. The surprise was that we too were under arrest. "What for?" I asked incredulously. "Harassing phone calls," was the answer.

.

You Must

They say you must hit rock bottom, before you will go up
You must fall all to pieces, before you find good luck
You must stare horror straight in its ugly face
Before you become happy, of sorrow you must taste
All these things I've been through, all that I have done
Were part of some big picture, of a future life to come
So, I prepare for hardship, and grow accustomed to its way
In hopes that come tomorrow, I can rise above today

CHAPTER 8

Inevitable Incarceration

MY GIRLFRIEND AND I SAT side by side in the magistrate's office while they typed up thirty warrants each for us, for every phone call she had made. I sat there in shock, but she started laughing hysterically and taunting the cops, telling them that thirty was not enough, could she have more please? My mind was mostly on Ron, because I didn't even fully understand why I was being charged, but Ron? He had nothing to do with any of it and had been at work when such things went on. I didn't see him again except briefly while we were being processed and fingerprinted back in the jail. During that time a group of cops came busting in with a prisoner that they were practically dragging. I looked up to see the bloody, beaten face of my sister's father. "Jvonne," he yelled, "help me. You're seeing this, call somebody, tell them they've beat me!" *Good Lord,* I thought, *what had he done?* Why had they beaten him? Why did it take five of them to manhandle him? It had been several years since I had seen ole Button, stepdad #1, and he was just as wiry and alcoholic skinny as I remembered. The jailer moved us fast so we couldn't see each other anymore and my one phone call had already been made, so there was nothing I could do for the man that had fathered my sister.

They set our bonds at $5000 each, and ran articles in the local newspaper about it as if they had discovered some sort of "satanic ring," even listing what to look for in your teen that might point to signs of devil worship! *Wow,* I thought, *this little one-horse town sure has its ass hat on backwards!* I might not have been very "Godly" at the time, but I most certainly never worshipped a "devil." Aiding and abetting harassing phone calls—that was what Ron and I were charged with. I wasn't sure how you could aid or abet a phone call. Technically speaking, the phone was in my name and I didn't report her for doing it, so that was my aiding and abetting, but Ron?

Miriam showed up within a couple of days to visit me in county jail. She offered to bail me out, which was tempting because I was scared in there and claustrophobic because of the small, dark, windowless cell. However, I knew Ron needed out more than I did because he had a job he could lose if he didn't get back to it. I think my staying and him getting out made an impression on my grandma who had sworn years before because of my dad that she would never put her house up as bail for anyone. But she came down and got me out anyway, and for that I was extremely grateful.

We had only been out on bail for a week, not even been to court yet for our first appearance, when on our way to pay our car insurance a patrol car passed us, whipped around and followed us. He accosted us in the parking lot before we could even go inside to pay our bill. The officer said we were under arrest again. Apparently, the plan was to issue a warrant for every phone call made, and there had been well over forty. I was confused because we had made bail once already. My rudimentary understanding of the law was that once you made bail, even if they added more charges you would most likely sign your own self out the second time, as bail was already covered. Not so in this Hubbard-hating den of authority. It became clear that it was the District Attorney who was pushing hardest about all this. He had been the DA for a good fifteen years. He saw my dad in and out of his courtroom, getting around heinous accusations time after time, year after year. It's unfortunate that he decided to dump all his bitterness and resentment of that fact onto my eighteen-year-old head! Seems he wanted to make an example out of me.

They did let Ron go on his own recognizance that second time around, but not me. They shoved me right back into that claustrophobic cell, with my "friend" who had never made bail the first time. Now it was she, I and two other grown women in that small four-bunk cell. One of the women was accused of having helped her murdering husband bury a body. Now, I'm no expert, but it seemed to me they should've put violent offenders somewhere other than in with children who had made harassing phone calls. It became a problem because the murderer's wife had taken a liking to my friend in my absence, and decided she would harass me. My friend would sit on the top bunk and rock back and forth laughing to herself. When I would ask her what was so damn funny, she would ask me if I could "hear it," "it" being voices she claimed she could hear, and since I couldn't I just sank back onto my bottom bunk. I wondered if she was really that far gone or faking some sort of mental illness in hopes it would help her in court?

The murderer's wife threatened me constantly in that cell, about how long my showers were, or how she might just choke me out in my sleep. A week went by and I was breaking down bad. I felt like I couldn't live another day confined like that. Then to my surprise and relief, my chiropractor, the one who had assisted me after the whiplash neck injury, came and put up my second bail. It should have meant something to those accusing me, that upstanding members of the community were putting up my bail, but it didn't.

It was two weeks until the first court date, and I had been given a court-appointed attorney who didn't even wear a suit. He wore blue jeans and long-sleeved flannel shirts, and looked a lot like "Grizzly Adams." I didn't dare go out anywhere during those two weeks, afraid a cop would spot me and arrest me again and have more warrants to add to their ever-growing collection. On my court date my last meal before going in was a barbeque sandwich with onion rings that my grandmother bought me for lunch at that same ole-time drugstore that I had stabbed a girl in front of. Ironically, here I was going to court for phone calls.

My attorney took me and Ron to a back room where he told us the DA had a deal for us: If I would go to prison for six months, they would drop all charges against Ron. Prison? What? Half a year? I couldn't fathom it. Why was this attorney not working for us? "That's too long," I said. He left the room and came back with the DA, who told me that five months was his final offer, and that if I didn't take it he would personally and aggressively pursue both Ron and me, and seek to send us both to prison for two years per warrant. Can you imagine that? That would've been like fifty-two years for making harassing phone calls! Surely that wasn't even legal or possible, however, I was eighteen and scared to death by how "unfair" the whole process had been thus far. I looked at Ron with tears in my eyes and he held my hands in his, with tears in his eyes, and I said, "Fine, I'll do the five months, to let Ron go free and get this over with."

For my transfer to prison I rode in the back of a police car between two male offenders, one a child molester, the other a boy I had gone to school with named Denver. Although Denver's current crime was theft, it was rumored that he had once been caught fucking a chicken! Many years later he would be accused of murdering a human being. Perhaps it's a slippery slope, from fucking chickens to murdering humans! Of course, my level of discomfort was at its highest handcuffed between the two of them for an eight-hour ride to the state capital. They dropped the males off first, then me.

The prison complex I went to was a minimum-security prison that was built like barracks. This helped me mentally with the amount of time I'd be there. I told myself this was just like basic training camp and I broke the months into weeks in my head to make it sound better. Nineteen weeks of basic training. I would mark a line through a week in my pocket calendar once it was done. There's not much in the world more degrading than having to get completely naked in front of a prison guard (albeit female) and squat and cough so they can make sure you aren't hiding anything in any of your orifices. I was quivering and near tears, but knew I couldn't let the other inmates see that sort of weak display. As the guard led me into the barracks of about fifty other women I felt like I would rather the earth swallow me than to live another day.

As I looked around I realized one thing fast: the population was at least 90 percent African American. I don't say this with any judgment on my part; rather I say it to confirm what most people already know about male prisons, and I affirm it to be true of the female prison as well. African Americans are incarcerated at a much higher rate than whites even though they are a minority in the population at large.

Guards in my barracks asked me what I was there for, and when I told them they laughed out loud. "Phone calls! Who goes to prison for phone calls?" *Yeah, I wish it had been that preposterous to those that sent me here,* I thought. The other inmates stared me down, some out of curiosity, others looking to establish their dominance or seniority. I was in regular population, and although it was a minimum-security prison, there were murderers, bank robbers, and vicious assailants in there, that had "good behaviored" themselves from maximum security to minimum. Some were doing life!

I got a top bunk, and my bunkmate was a black woman who displayed attitude with me almost from the get go. I was terrified on the inside. She complained about every move I made on the bed, and rickety as they were, it was impossible not to feel movement with the slightest repositioning. One day we were all on our bunks to be counted and she started up on me. "I swear if you don't stop moving up there, I am going to make it so you never move again!" she said. It's funny how time stands still in moments where you must decide something as monumental as whether to talk back to your potential assailant or submit and be scared and nervous all the time. I figured I had no choice but to gamble on standing up for myself, so I responded with, "Well, why don't you just bring your ass on up here and we'll see how that works out for you." Everyone else in the barracks heard this exchange, but since the guard had entered to count us there was only silence until the guard was gone. Then my bunkmate stood up, to kill me I was sure, but instead she put her hand out to me and said, "It's about time girl, we were a little worried about whether you'd make it in here or not." Was this a joke? Was she going to shank me with the other arm? Or had I watched too many prison movies? I took her hand and she shook mine and said, "I think you'll be all right, Pollyanna." I honestly at the time didn't know who Pollyanna was, but that, as well as Alice (for *Alice in Wonderland*) became my prison nicknames, I guess just for being so damned white and blonde!

I had decided there was no room for self-pity. I may not have deserved to be there because of harassing phone calls, but I accepted that I did deserve to be there, for all I had done that was never proven (flattening tires, busting headlights, spray-painting houses). Receiving letters from back home was about all anyone had to look forward to. On days you didn't get any mail it was rather depressing. As I got to know my fellow inmates better I started to see a pattern. Women, especially black women, get much harsher sentences for their crimes than most men do. There was one eighteen-year-old dainty little black girl in for life, for murder, even though the person she had "murdered" had been an intruder in her home. She had shot him in the back as he tried to retreat. Another black lady in her mid-thirties, who had five children, one of whom she had been pregnant with at the time of incarceration, was in for life for the murder of her domestically violent husband. Apparently after years and years of abuse he hit her while she was pregnant and she had enough and blew him away! She had to give birth to that last baby in prison and then have it ripped from her arms and taken away. There was a Native American woman in for murder, who had been a clerk at a convenience store when it was held up. Once the thief had robbed her she shot him dead as he tried to run away. Now she was doing life. The stories went on and on, and yeah, I know everybody in prison is "innocent," but that is not what I mean. They weren't claiming not to have done what they were accused of doing, rather just questioning whether true justice had been served by the severity of the sentences. My opinion on the aforementioned examples was no. A lot of the women were there on drug and/or prostitution charges. Then as now, I question how it helps at all to incarcerate such women rather than seek to rehabilitate them. I know personally that shooting them with a pellet pistol doesn't help!

I was lucky in that while I was there, an outside community college granted a chosen few the chance of a higher education. They had a Certified Nurse's Assistant training program for non-violent offenders. The program was almost as long as my sentence. In addition to the classroom we were eventually taken outside the prison to a nursing home to assist nurses in a hands-on environment. At the end of the program we had a graduation ceremony and were presented our certifications. Miriam drove all the way from back home, an eight-hour trip, to be there for that. God bless that woman and all she tried to do for me.

By the end of my sentence, I had grown quite fond of several ladies whose whole lives would play out in that prison. I thought about how lucky I was to be going home as I rode a Greyhound, via a prison-paid bus ticket. I was hungry with no money for what would turn into a twelve-hour trip, given transfers. On the second bus however, I met a Marine who was on his way to the beach for vacation. He sat beside me and flirted madly, eventually even offering to take me with him to his vacation destination. I was flattered, and giving where I was coming from, very tempted. The cold hard truth though couldn't be ignored. I had to report to my probation officer within twenty-four hours of release. I told the guy the truth—that I was coming from incarceration—and he was still nice enough to buy me a meal at the next station.

Home was a dumpy trailer right next to my dad that Ron had managed to rent in my absence. We had lost the apartment upon my incarceration. It was strange to be back, mostly because nothing except me had changed. Life looked bleak as usual, and I had come to the conclusion that real love did not exist. I didn't want to go back to my old life. I wanted out! I started out with all the right intentions. Got a job at a nursing home as a CNA. Gave up on being any sort of criminal because prison was not a place I planned on ever seeing the inside of again, especially considering I had been taunted by one guard that I'd be back, because "they all come back." However, change is hard when everyone around you is still in the muck trying to suck you into their despair.

Soon after I came home my stepmom left my dad; his response was to start drinking again. It was around Christmas time, so he took his Christmas tree outside and set it on fire, built a beer can pyramid on his kitchen table, and accidentally ran over his own dog coming back from the beer store. I'm telling you, it was a tragic country song come to life.

My job at the nursing home, which was one county over from where I lived, only lasted about a month. I loved working with the elderly. They were sweet and often filled with great stories from so much life experience. My biggest problem, according to the head nurse, was that I took too much time with my patients doing things for them like cutting their nails, brushing their hair, or just talking to them. According to her, all I had time to do was wipe and go! About a month in, she told me I needed to know the signs of a do-not-resuscitate dying patient. She took me into one of her patient rooms where a lady was dying slowly by what seemed like suffocation given the noises she was making. Horrible gurgling sounds were escaping her throat as she gasped for air. I froze up inside; I couldn't stand it. When I went on lunch break, I couldn't eat; all I could think about was how I couldn't stand to see that happen over and over, and possibly to the patients I was growing close to, and so I never went back from that lunch break. Instead I cruised up and down main street, eventually making my way to the mall just to walk around and waste time until Ron got off from his job. I know it may seem hard to believe given the content of my life thus far, but that's when things took a turn for the worse.

Holding Evil's Hand

Evil has a face, one I had forgotten
Its soul is dark and tragic, its heart is old and rotten
Intentions full of harm, brought about with pain
A hidden sort of laughter, meant to drive your soul insane
Becoming so confused, blindly you stumble forth
To find the hand you're holding, to be the one you should
divorce
In its final hour, harder does it fight
To fill your head with ugly thoughts, and fill your heart
with fright
With ghostly apparitions, and visions in your head
Convincing you it's over, that soon you will be dead
Harder must you look, if you ever hope to see
That you might have let the evil in, like a dreadful, sick
disease
Only faith will save you, stronger will it stand
When you free yourself the bondage, of ever holding
evil's hand

CHAPTER 9

Domestic Violence

LIFE HELD LITTLE JOY FOR me. It had been too damn hard for far too long, and I was tired of hoping it would ever get better. I was tired of everybody I knew being a drunk, a troublemaker or low life. I knew there had to be more to life. I just needed to find another way.

On my way into the mall I locked eyes with a guy driving through the parking lot in a nice little foreign car. He smiled at me, but I just kept walking. At the mall, I met a chick working in the leather store who was friendly and interesting and so after she got off work we drove downtown to Main Street where local youths cruised and parked to socialize. During our cruising, I passed that same guy from the mall parking lot; again he smiled at me. As we made our way to a parking spot, he followed, got out and started trying to talk me up. I was cold and stiff with him at first. He wasn't my type at all, not looks-wise, interest-wise or anything, but I wasn't taking any of it seriously anyway, because I had a boyfriend. This guy wanted my phone number and to avoid that I told him to just give me his, thinking I would trash it later.

I jotted it down, and with him being unsuccessful in moving me one way or the other, he left.

Now just when you thought it couldn't get any weirder, it did. My mother had written me one letter while I was in prison, claiming she had heard what happened and wanted to reconnect. Also, it seems she was having trouble once more with my stepdad Wade. When she came around to visit me and found out my stepmom had left my dad, they started spending time together. I was nineteen, and *now* my mom and dad were going to get back together? Oh, but it didn't stop there. My dad couldn't pay his rent with my stepmom gone, so after just a couple of weeks he moved in with my mom and sister! Close on the heels of that, Ron and I were so far behind in paying the costs of living in our rented trailer, that we also moved in with my mom. Five people living in a two-bedroom trailer!

I don't know what Ron was thinking as far as any future for us but I pretty much decided to ignore how pathetic life was and try to have fun. I started going out on the weekends with the girl from the mall. She was a hippie chick who smoked pot and drank when she could get her hands on alcohol. I did neither of those things, but since it looked like everyone else on the planet did I tried not to let it bias me against being her friend. We would go to dance clubs just wanting to dance freely by ourselves. So, we started going to a gay bar instead where we could dance without all the horn dogs hounding us! A few times we were turned away at the door because they could tell my friend was already drunk, and being underage, that wasn't going to fly. Other times I had to hold her hair back while she puked. Often while out in public she would just ask random people if they had a joint, which I thought was risky behavior. I guess I felt like I had to watch over her to keep her safe. Now, the guy from the mall and cruising who gave me his number often showed up wherever she and I went. His name was Warren. He was relentless in his pursuit of me, no matter if I was stone cold or warm enough to let him buy me something to eat. He even knew I had a boyfriend, but nothing seemed to stop him from showing up.

Ron and I had grown apart, and he was getting as tired of my behavior as I was tired of our life in general. I think we stayed together out of financial necessity more than anything at this point. Neither of us had anywhere else to go. Ron thought I was cheating on him, which I was not, in any sexual way. However, considering that I wouldn't completely tell this other guy to get permanently lost wasn't exactly normal. I suppose even though I liked nothing about this new guy I was under the impression that he might be going somewhere in life that was better than what I had known life to be. He was tall, blond, blue eyed, and I suppose handsome to many females. Well dressed, clean cut and driving a brand new little Mitsubishi. The way he talked always seemed arrogant and irritating to me. It infuriated me further that everyone but me seemed to think he was the greatest thing ever. "What a nice, clean-cut boy," my grandma once commented. She had always thought little of Ron's long black hair and heavy metal t-shirts, even though I knew below the surface which one was the better person. Warren seemed to know which flavor of charming to be, depending on whom he was trying to impress.

Ron, however, was getting sick of it all, and so I told Warren to stay away from me. I told him that the day he had shown up in the parking lot of Ron's job, which was a factory out in the middle of nowhere on land that had once been pig farming territory. That night, several hours later, when I came back to pick Ron up, we were driving down the dark country road away from the factory when out of the bushes along the side of the road Warren jumped out into the middle of the highway and scared the shit out of us! I swerved around him and accelerated. "What the fuck?" Ron and I both said out loud, and simultaneously. It was bizarre, to have someone jump out of the pitch-black darkness into oncoming traffic! Had he been waiting all day in that brush for me? I sure as hell didn't stop, because it was late and we had a long drive from Ron's job to my mom's where we were staying.

We were about twenty minutes into our forty-minute drive when we began to hear sirens in the distance. I kept looking in the rearview mirror around every treacherous mountain curve, wondering where those sirens were coming from. Suddenly, a car came up behind us dangerously fast. It pulled around me in a curve and nearly ran me off the road. In the rearview mirror the blue lights became visible. The sirens belonged to three police cars in hot pursuit of the maniac behind the wheel of the car that just nearly sideswiped us.

At first, we tried to keep up with the police chase because I was angry that whomever they were pursuing nearly wrecked us. We lost sight of the lights for a while, but eventually caught up to them. Oddly enough they had turned down the road we lived on. Then we saw the car that passed us in the ditch, with the driver's side door hanging open. We pulled over and got out to ask the police what was going on. As we were standing there I glimpsed some sort of object lying in the road. Ron was telling the officer how we were almost run off the road by their culprit. The police officer was saying they didn't even know who they were chasing, only that the car had been stolen from a supermarket parking lot and that whoever had been driving had ditched it and run into the thick woods surrounding the area. That's when the object in the road crystallized before my eyes, and my body shivered all through. "It's his hat," I stammered. "Whose hat?" asked Ron and the cop at the same time. I moved closer to the object and shuddered, because it really was his hat. "Warren," I stammered. "That's his hat."

Now the police had a name, they knew who to look for so they brought dogs to search the woods. Ron and I went on home, where we filled my mom and dad in on the ruckus. No one slept that night, either from the sound of the hounds hunting, or the voices of police shouting out in those woods. At daylight, there came a knock on the door. Warren was standing outside, shivering from the morning cold. My dad talked to him through the locked door as I called the police to alert them that he was there. He said he was hungry, so my dad fixed him a sandwich and then asked him to step back into the driveway. Then Dad opened the door a crack and sat the sandwich on the porch. As Warren stood there eating the sandwich, the police approached him on foot with guns drawn. He simply sat the plate down and with no attempt to resist was handcuffed and taken away.

It's odd how all this affected everyone differently. Ron moved out and in with a mutual male friend of ours. My dad seemed to feel sorry for Warren. I suppose criminals must stick together. My mom was terrified for everyone's safety. I was confused. Maybe that's why I took that collect call from the county jail later. I did at least want to hear what Warren had been thinking to do such a thing. In that phone call, he told me that he was crazy about me. He insisted that I was all he could think of and that when I had told him to go away and that I never wanted to see him again that he had been heartbroken. Further, when he had jumped out at us from the bushes trying to wave me down and I just kept going he had hitched a ride with another employee of that factory to the nearest grocery store. He had found a car running outside the store and with what he called love-sickened, temporary insanity had stolen the car trying to get to me. Before that call was finished, he had me believing that it was my fault he had stolen the car, and now he sat in jail, just for loving someone so much.

I'd like to say that all that sounded sick to me and a part of it did, but then I wasn't all that together myself. Without ever seeing the parallel or how quickly I acted just like my mother, I became Warren's girlfriend as soon as he got out of jail. Now, this relationship was tumultuous from the get go. "Crazy over me" was just an excuse for crazy in general. I don't know how many times we argued or how many times we fought because it was the constant state of our relationship. He would threaten suicide if I talked of breaking up and once he saw that work it became his go-to plan for keeping me, lying down in the highway waiting to get run over, or saying he would hang himself, shoot himself or attempt to overdose. At nineteen years old, still very much a naive girl, I was horrified by these claims and would back down, not wanting to be "responsible" for someone's death. Warren was twenty-five years old, supposedly already a man.

Then before too long, I was pregnant, something I thought I never wanted to be. Before the first ultrasound even, I was married, something I knew I never wanted to be. To wrap your head around all this you would have had to be as empty, numb and dead on the inside as I was about life and love in general. It didn't much matter, I figured, because happiness wasn't for people like me and love did not really exist. At least, I had never seen it. Pregnancy was awful! For one I was sick 24/7, not just in the mornings and not normal sick, but hospitalized and fed through the veins due to dehydration and malnutrition. It was then, in my weakest state that my now husband began to abuse me in all sorts of new and more frightful ways. In a short period he went from bad to evil, and we're talking the sort of evil that crime shows tell stories about. Pulling me out of the car by one leg and dragging me across the yard while I was pregnant. Stealing my purse and running away with it, with me chasing him while pregnant. Yanking me out of the car another time by the wrists and throwing me to the pavement to take off with my car and abandon me. It was constant stress, constant anxiety, and constant violence.

I went into premature labor at twenty-four-and-a-half weeks along, when my placenta started to separate. I was passing pure blood for urine. I was told over the phone by the ob-gyn who was supposed to deliver my baby that there was no way a baby could live at this stage of pregnancy. Then he added, if I wanted to have the best chance I would need to be rushed to a hospital two counties over from where we lived. Knowing I could not handle losing my baby, of course I went the distance to Asheville, NC where Memorial Mission had a neonatal intensive care unit. The rest of that day was a manic blur. Rushed in on a gurney, horrible pain in my low back, prepping for C-section, weighing the baby while it was still inside me, me crying, epidural, fear, and then one faint noise . . . "aaah." It was a boy, and he was alive; I heard him. They held him up and ran to get him on a ventilator. He could not breathe on his own; his lungs were barely formed. He was almost transparent. You could see veins and blood vessels through his pale, underdeveloped skin. He was put on life support and still enough oxygen was lost at birth that he would by age two be diagnosed with cerebral palsy. However, cerebral palsy was the least of my worries then.

Five days after giving birth I had hit the bathroom floor, thinking my stitches had ripped internally there was so much pain. I was rushed to a different hospital than my baby was in and discovered to have a huge kidney stone. However, my iron level was too low to remove it, so I had a stent surgically inserted into my ureter to bypass the stone until I could have it surgically removed. I was in so much physical pain the nurses at the neonatal ICU begged me to just go home and rest. Rest? I don't think I had done that in ten years and my circumstances sure weren't conducive to that now. So, I just pushed on; there was nothing else to do but that.

For five months, my baby stayed in that neonatal intensive care unit, making a regular habit out of almost dying, having further complications that required emergency surgeries, being put into a medically induced coma so as not to move around too much and cause his heart rate to destabilize. All through that five-month nightmare I pretty much lived at the hospital, and quite literally in the waiting room for three months, as we were homeless. Why? Because nothing about my suffering or his own baby almost dying changed anything about the way Warren operated.

We had been living with his grandparents in the basement of their two-story home. His grandfather was disabled and in a wheelchair. One day while getting ready to go back to the hospital to be with the baby I heard cussing and yelling. I came up from the basement to find Warren at the bottom level of the stairs screaming at his grandfather who was sitting in his wheelchair at the top of the stairs. Then to my shock and horror Warren ran up the steps at full speed and knocked his grandfather over and out of his wheelchair. I screamed, his grandma screamed and Warren just pulled me out of the house and shoved me into the car. He wouldn't explain anything, just drove like a maniac to his parents' house, which was an hour's drive away. When we got there, no one was home. Warren just kicked in their front door and scrambled around their bedroom stealing his dad's firearms. I was beyond terrified. The fact he had assaulted his own handicapped grandfather and stolen his dad's guns was horrifying enough, but then he dropped me off at the hospital and disappeared for a solid week, all during his baby's fight for life. In that week, he totaled the only vehicle we had and when he showed back up, although he was arrested nothing came of it. His grandparents wouldn't press charges and the firearms were not to be found, so there was no proof to the complaint his dad had made. I just kept my mouth shut and head down and spent hour upon hour at the bed-side of my fragile premature baby.

I named my son Monte and he was four months old before I ever got to hold him; to have done so any sooner could have killed him. He was by all accounts a miracle baby, but he was more than that to me. He was my savior. Motherhood will change a woman, or it should anyway because no longer could I just stumble through life not quite caring. In fact, now for the first time ever in my life I had something more important than myself to worry about. For the first time in my life I knew unconditional, true and unshakable love. When Monte finally got to come home it was with oxygen and a heart monitor and a plethora of health problems. The first two years of his life were nothing but hospital horrors. Seven pneumonia hospitalizations, one RSV (a deadly respiratory virus), endless BPD (a chronic respiratory illness). Yet in between the baby's horrors and health scares the unstable marriage continued, as well as the abuse. If anything, it intensified.

I was changed forever by having an innocent little life to look after, but Warren was not. There was a lot of abuse going on at home and only now were my family members starting to realize what a dangerous situation I was in. Long gone were the idle threats of suicide. Warren made it clear repeatedly who would die now if I ever tried to leave him. I was held in place by my most precious possession, my son. I was told things like: If you ever try to leave me, I will hunt you down and kill you and Monte both, or I will kidnap the baby and you will never see him again. I had seen him commit violence on others and had felt him commit violence on me. I had every reason to believe I was trapped.

The roller coaster that was my married life led us back to having to live with my parents or his. We would go back and forth between the two based on whoever was last to throw us out again due to Warren's unstable and violent behavior. It was during one of our stints at my parents, when Monte was just a few months old, that Warren put what I thought was a loaded pistol into his own mouth and pulled the trigger. When nothing happened, he ran with the gun and drove away in our car. A couple of hours passed with me just sitting in a state of shock and worry. Then he called me on the phone and was breathing heavy, crying and carrying on. He claimed he had just shot his own grandmother, and that she was lying in his arms at that moment, bleeding to death! I believed him so much that I hung up and called the police and told them what he had claimed. They went to the grandmother's address to find her alive and well and not even having heard from him. They looked for Warren all evening, but eventually he came back and parked at the end of my parents' driveway. I called the police to alert them. Within a few short minutes, multiple patrol cars pulled up and about five officers, three with guns drawn, approached him in his vehicle. The policemen were shouting, "Put your hands on the dashboard where we can see them!" I was watching from a window inside the trailer, almost sure they were going to have to shoot him. He was armed, dangerous and had made extreme claims that warranted the police behavior. Upon their recommendation, I had local authorities commit him to a mental hospital but he was released within two weeks. I will never forget his cold, evil, dire warning after returning from the mental institution. "I will find a way to get even with you that will destroy you!" It would take a full year for that to come around and once it did it was so horrible that I did the only thing I could do at the time, which was not believe it.

My husband Warren raped my nine-year-old sister. This rape claim played out very chaotic. It was a he said, she said sort of thing and the she saying it most was my mom, which is why I wasn't keen on believing it. After all, she had been one of the first in my life to hurt and betray me. Now that she hated my husband, and given her own track record, I wasn't sure she wasn't just trying to stir up trouble. Even though he was arrested and charged his parents hired him attorneys and the next thing I knew it was dismissed from court. No trial. No jury. Nothing. I never really knew why. At the time, I figured it was because he didn't do it. After all, I had not been able to speak to my sister about it, because my mom acted as a suspicious shield between her and anyone with questions. Total estrangement from all family ensued as shortly after Warren ran over his own mother's foot with a Chevy Blazer in an attempt to run her over during one of his outbursts. So, he was eluding arrest in his home state of South Carolina for assault with a deadly weapon with intent to kill. Also, questionable rape charges still loomed for him there as it had been a two-time thing, the rape.

Monte and myself? We were just trying to survive day to day. Between the 2 a.m. rides from hell the wrong way down the interstate at a hundred-plus miles per hour, claiming we were all going to die together, and threats of burning the house down while we slept in it, there wasn't a lot of down time for contemplating whether the bastard was also a rapist or not. Numb, cold, dead inside and just waiting to be murdered, I was starting to believe that God was dead!

Since Warren would not hold a job, I started considering some things that had interested me in my teens. Movie extra, wrestling valet, and eventually magician's assistant. Yes, on a local level, I had myself a dabble in entertainment. It was one of the photographers I had worked with who told me about the magician's assistant job. I remember when I called the magician to set up an interview he sounded very peculiar. Something was odd about his voice. It sounded like a weird mixture of cartoonish and ghoulish. When I met him, the voice turned out to be a product of the fact that he was physically handicapped. He had a rare bone disease that left him almost completely disabled. Nothing about his handicap scared me. It amazed me even more that he sat there in his own magic shop running the whole show! The magician quickly became my best friend. I had never met anyone as funny, or as fun, as he was. He and I clicked on a level that I had never experienced before. Despite his debilitated frame, he was the strongest person I had ever met. He spoke with confidence and authority on matters of a higher power. He spoke the language that I remembered God speaking to my heart long before life had left me bitter. In a short period of time, our strongest bond was God, and the magician was my spiritual "guru" of sorts

Monte and I would travel with him to magic shows and conventions, and before long I loved him more than I had ever been able to love most of my family. He was the only person who ever "stood up" to my evil husband. Once when we had a magic show to do, Warren was in the yard trying to take a part off the car to disable it so I couldn't go. I jumped in barefooted with Monte strapped in the back car seat and drove quickly to fulfill my duties in that performance. After the show when the magician, Monte and I got back to the magic shop, Warren was waiting there. He began to shout at me and cuss and threaten. Then from his place in the passenger seat with the door open, the magician reached out and tweaked Warren's nose as he was shouting. I held my breath for a moment, stunned. I just knew Warren was going to punch him, but he didn't. It stunned Warren too and for a moment he was quiet before pulling me away, shoving me and Monte into our car and driving away. How very bold and daring, I thought. This little handicapped man with all his limitations had just driven a monster away, albeit temporarily! The magician witnessed a lot of things about my personal life during the last three years of my marriage that I know angered him and worried him for my and Monte's safety. I will forever be grateful for his being in my life at a time when there was seemingly no hope.

Even though Warren had moved us all the way to Sevierville, TN, to elude arrest, he was eventually caught driving without a license and sent back to South Carolina for the assault with a deadly weapon (the car), with intent to kill (his mom). As always though, they dropped the charges and he was free to continue his reign of torment against me. He moved us back to South Carolina to be closer to his family again. I continued to do the traveling magic shows though.

One thing that I always tried to do for my baby Monte, even though we lived in poverty, was keep a bank account for him. After all, it was his disability check that usually paid our rent, because as I said Warren wouldn't keep a job. It wasn't much, maybe $20 to $30 a month but I was determined to try and save something for this child's future, whatever it was going to be. I don't know how many times or how many banks I had moved this money around in but it was a lot. Why? Because for one I had tried to keep it a secret from Warren. Then we would go back and forth on his name being on the account along with mine, to just back to mine, to both of ours again. Whenever I felt threatened I would run to the bank, close the account, go to a new bank and open an account Warren couldn't touch.

It was early 1999 when while living in a substandard dump, Warren and I began to fight over something and he sped off in the car. He drove all the way to Tennessee to "kill" a guy he thought I had an affair with. Said guy was a nice fellow I had met while we had been living in Tennessee. We had worked together at a restaurant where I waitressed during that time. I had left quite a few of my most personal possessions with this fellow for safekeeping, when Warren had moved us back to South Carolina. In the back of my mind I held out hope of finding a window that would allow me to leave this insane bastard! Warren called me a few hours later to tell me he had all my stuff in the car and was on his way back with it. I hung up the phone and cried in defeat. Then it hit me. *Oh shit, my baby's money!* It was in a South Carolina bank, in an account that had both my and Warren's names on it. I just knew he would make that his first stop the moment he got back from Tennessee. What could I do? He had the car. The bank was at least fifteen miles from the shithole we were living in. I stopped crying. *No, I will not let this happen,* I thought. I strapped four-year-old Monte into his stroller and headed out to the four-lane highway (that had no safety sidewalks). I ran along the side of the highway pushing that stroller, stopping only briefly to catch my breath and then set off again.

I was about five miles in when I stopped at a convenience store. Breathless and afraid that I could never beat Warren to the bank, I spotted an ole country fella heading toward his pickup truck. Desperate, I asked him for a ride the rest of the way to the bank. He was more than glad to help. He put the stroller in the bed of his truck while Monte and I hopped in the front seat. I thanked him as he let us off at the bank. I went inside and a teller began to help me with the closing process. I told her that it was urgent, as I feared my husband would stop at the closest branch on his way back and try to do the same. Mid-process she could see on her computer that someone was indeed at another branch trying to close out the account. Bless that lady, she called the other branch and explained to the teller on the other end what was going on. Stopping his attempt, she handed the contents of the account to me. It was close to $1,000 by then. With money in hand I started pushing that stroller as fast as my legs would carry me towards another bank about a mile down the street. I was nearly there when I heard screeching tires approaching. Warren was flying down the road towards me and he looked pissed. He swerved the car into a driveway and got out, approaching me quickly, but I screamed "Help me!" and ran towards a man in his backyard who had heard the ruckus. Cowards like Warren, who beat up women, rape children and torment family usually go into self-preservation mode when you try to involve other people. He tried to change his demeanor so the stranger wouldn't intervene. However, I bolted the last few steps inside the bank and sat down at a desk to open a new account. Warren followed me in but he couldn't make a scene in a bank. He had to sit there and just watch and listen as I put my baby's money into an account with just my name on it. I knew I would pay some other way later, but at least he didn't get the baby's money!

Then something finally happened one day, something I wish had happened a lot sooner. I decided that dying could not be as bad as continuing to live life as it was. It's strange how instantaneous it was. The stage was set for another round of torture. It was close to midnight, Monte was strapped safe in his car seat in the backseat. Warren and I were arguing and he was getting heated and crazy. I was driving. He punched the windshield and caused it to crack all the way across. He had done that to at least three different vehicles during our five-year marriage. This time though, instead of screaming or crying I started laughing hysterically. Warren looked puzzled as we were exiting the interstate via a ramp. At the light as I kept laughing, he said, "That's it, I'm going to kill myself! I will jump off that bridge" pointing to the high overpass just across from the light. I stopped laughing, reached across him and opened the passenger door from the inside. Stoic and broken I said, "Have at it." He looked incredulous, like I couldn't be serious, but then sprang from the car and ran across the highway and jumped up on the overpass. Just then the light turned green, and I made my way towards him. He stood there on that overpass, waiting I know for my usual pleas of "No please don't do this," but instead, I drove right past him. I looked in the rearview mirror and the moment I passed by, he got down. I'd be lying if I didn't say I wish he had lost his footing and slipped on down to become bug shit on a semi-truck, but on the other hand it occurred to me: What if, just like his suicide threats, the death threats were all a bluff? So I kept on driving, although I began to hyperventilate from the stress of it all.

I stopped by a local fire department to tell them about him and the overpass, in case they wanted to check it out and in case he had changed his mind and done the world a favor. Then I drove across the state line and made it to my mom and sister's house in North Carolina. I had not seen them in over two years, since the rape allegations. My dad had long since left them and was currently living in a camper beside my grandma Hubbard's house. I spent the next two years just trying to recover from all that had happened during my six years married to a lunatic.

The Bloom

Time stands still, completely, totally
It's like sitting and staring at an un-bloomed flower
Waiting, watching and the more you look, the more you
cannot see
The flower seems the same, never changing
Is it because you watch it so much?
And if you go away for only a day, it will bloom while you
are gone and when you return to see that it has blossomed
Your joy falls to the ground, as its petals wilt before your
eyes.
Odd how he could never thrive before you,
but has no shame in letting you watch him die.

Written: October 1994

In reference to the struggles of my son Monte's premature
birth

CHAPTER 10

Monte and the Magician

ONCE, WHEN MONTE WAS JUST two and a half years old, from the backseat of the car he said, "Heaven is like a courtroom; there are twelve judges." Another time, when he was four, he was with me in a store when he discovered a greeting card rack and I found him standing there staring at it. When I asked him what he was looking at, he pointed and asked me if he could have "that picture of God." Following his finger, my eyes rested upon this greeting card that had a figure bathed in bright white light on the front, standing in a garden of flowers. You couldn't make out any details of the face, or whether this being was male or female. It was just peacefully standing there emanating a bright white light.

The purity and conviction of his statements blew me away. I wondered where Monte had been all those months as a premature baby. Lying there on a ventilator, with tubes in his chest and down his throat. Eyes wide open for a month straight, while in a medically-induced coma. He didn't appear to be there with his body during that time. It felt like he was gone and had left behind a little baby shell. He was somewhere though, perhaps on a level or plane that held him safe and secure while his tiny body endured so much.

As he grew, so did his wit and understanding. I swear, at five years old you could literally explain anything to him, and he got it. He conversed like a tiny adult, never complained and always brought me joy. He was a part of everything I did, including traveling with the magician for shows and conventions. Before I had gotten away from his biological father, Monte had already started to try and stand up for me, even though he was barely four. If his dad grabbed him up to carry him to the car every vein in his neck would stand out as he screamed, "I wish you would just go back to jail!" He wanted nothing to do with him and he would often tell him to "just go away."

When we did get away I hoped it was soon enough to not damage Monte in any lasting or permanent way. At first, and for maybe a year after we left, Monte would say he saw a dark man. Sometimes in his room, maybe outside his window, and once even out in the middle of the ocean while we were on one of our magic show trips. It was odd because he would stare out and into something very deeply. For my part, it took at least two years for me to stop watching all headlights in my rearview mirror, fearing Warren was coming to kill us.

During those two years, the magician, Monte and I lived half the time in hotel rooms while we traveled for magic shows and conventions. It was in one of those hotel rooms that I sat with the phone and did something I considered necessary. I tried to make amends to all the people I felt I had hurt, either directly or by way of Warren's behavior over the years. The first person I called was my grandma Hubbard. I had not seen or spoken to her in over a year. Warren had me so isolated and far removed from any support during our marriage, Grandma had fallen by the wayside. She was so happy to hear I had gotten away from him. During our conversation I asked her if she could look up Miriam's phone number for me. Sadly, she told me Miriam had been in a car wreck just a few months before and had passed away. I was distraught at such news. Grandma went on to say that she had called and spoken to Miriam's husband during that time to offer condolences. According to her, he had seemed bitter about me, feeling my behavior had been hurtful and disappointing to Miriam.

I got off the phone and cried like a baby. I would never get to make amends with her in this lifetime. I was so overwhelmed with grief that I started trying to find out via public record where she was buried, so that I could go to the gravesite. In my searching, I found out she had been cremated, without burial. The magician tried to console me, while I lay on that hotel bed and cried until my eyes were near swollen shut. That night I had a dream. In the dream, Miriam came to me and told me she knew I was sorry and that she forgave me. She took my hand, through an open car window, held it for a moment and then was gone. I awoke with a start, then cried some more to realize it had only been a dream. Perhaps though, God sent me that dream and Miriam through it, so that I could move forward.

Also, I began calling around trying to track down Ron. Bless his heart, if anyone I had ever hurt deserved an apology more than he, I wasn't aware of it. Luckily, through his father I was able to track him down. I half-figured Ron might tell me to go straight to hell, but he didn't. Surprisingly, he was glad to hear from me and we even managed to laugh a time or two during our conversation. Afterwards, I think I slept for the better part of two days. I was so emotionally drained.

The magician didn't pay me a salary, because he was feeding and sheltering Monte and me at least half the time. He had also helped me get a vehicle of my own. The other half of the time I was in Tennessee. The nice fellow who had once allowed me to leave my stuff with him was more than willing to let Monte and I stay with him some. He was a very quiet, shy, non-threatening guy who had taken a liking to me. Now that I was free from the demon that had controlled my life, I started seeing this guy in Tennessee. So half the week in North Carolina traveling with the magician, the other half of the week, staying in Tennessee. I was terribly confused, traumatized, exhausted and afraid. I just wanted to feel safe. I wanted to keep Monte safe. I stayed on the move on purpose to prevent Warren from finding and killing us.

I filed divorce papers giving me full custody. The local newspaper ran the info, giving Warren due time to respond. After a month of no response from him, however, I was granted divorce. I wanted more security than that though, so I filed papers to have him parentally terminated forever. Once again, the info ran in the local newspaper, no response from the now ex-husband, and so it was that Monte was free also. Free from even being considered his child. Next, I paid attorneys to have Monte's last name changed to my maiden name, Hubbard. At last, I had eradicated the evil from our lives, legally!

As I tried to recover day by day from the horrors that such a dysfunctional marriage had left me with, men continued to give me trouble. It was a different kind of trouble mind you, but I suppose men will be men, no matter the circumstances. Even though I loved the magician, and would have tried my best to take care of him, had he suddenly been without family, I never thought of our relationship as romantic. Actually, it was greater than that, although he never liked hearing that. I realize I had put him on a pedestal, making him almost Godlike in my mind. Being with him was like being in the presence of God and therefore I never saw him as a romantic partner. I knew he loved me too, but I had always hoped it was in that same way. It was not. Apparently, he had always assumed that if I ever got away from the crazy husband that he and I would be together permanently. When he found out I was seeing someone in Tennessee he became extremely jealous and even angry with me. He withdrew from me and we went almost a year without seeing or speaking to each other. I thought about him a lot, and it broke my heart to not have him in my life, but I couldn't force feelings I didn't have.

The separation caused him pain too and so we reunited for about another year. That year was fraught with discomfort however because he persisted down the avenue of trying to be more than I wanted him to be. It culminated with him trying to get physical with me when I lay down to sleep. He wanted to touch me, and although I could feel his energy and his love I did not want a sexual relationship with him. In the end he allowed that to sever our friendship forever. The saddest part about it is that he actually went through a period of feeling used. Maybe he had to be angry at me, in order to keep from hurting, but he said hurtful things to me, implying that I had used him. Looking back, I'll admit I lived a certain way with him, but only because he insisted. He plied me with dinners out, took care of my vehicle maintenance when we were on the road, and sometimes would hand me a credit card and tell me to use it for whatever I needed. The lifestyle he lived as a magician seemed to suggest these things were normal, and I was in no mental or emotional state to discriminate between normal and abnormal.

The shows were fun though. We always had a blast! He had a version of the 'saw a girl in half' where the girl takes revenge and lights his top hat on fire. Part of our gimmick was that afterwards I would stumble across stage with a fire extinguisher and proceed like a "dumb blonde" to try and read the instructions, scratching my head all the while. Once, during a convention performance of this act, I lit his hat on fire as usual. By the end of our shtick though I knew something was wrong. Something had gone wrong with the hat and the fire had actually burned through and caused a quarter-sized hole into his head. He hadn't given one indication while on stage that anything was going wrong. So dedicated to his art he was, that he had sat through a burning head until the performance conclusion!

I also had a blast during our time together while dabbling in wrestling. I had been picked by a local wrestling promotion to serve as a manager/valet to a wrestler known as K. C. Thunder. He was a "bad guy," so of course my job was to rake the eyes and kick the stomachs of all the opponents he threw outside the ring. The magician would travel with Monte and me for those performances as well. About six months in I transferred over to a bald wrestler known as Bonamo Joe. My gimmick with him was to follow him out to the ring brushing his nonexistent hair. I guess I should have taken it as a compliment to my acting abilities when a couple of rowdy, obese, female fans started heckling me. "He ain't got no hair, you stupid bitch!," they would yell from the sidelines. However, these same women followed this wrestling promotion from town to town and eventually their taunts got so angry and fraught with threats that I had to come out with security behind me. Then it happened once that they spat on me from the front row and without hesitation or a moment to think, I spat right back. Apparently, that was frowned upon and so I was let go. It was okay though, I didn't need that abuse. The wrestling didn't pay squat anyway. Not enough to possibly get shanked by a deluded fan in the parking lot!

I even had a small opportunity to be an extra in a movie called *My Fellow Americans*, which they shot part of at the Biltmore Estate in Asheville, NC. It was exciting as I got to meet and take pictures with Dan Aykroyd, James Garner and John Heard while on the set.

In other areas of my life, I was trying to take the bull by the horns and face my demons. One of those areas, of course, was my dad. In fact, on his birthday in 2001, I went to visit him back in Brevard. I had gotten him a western-style bolo tie. He was already drunk when I arrived for my visit and shortly after me getting there he asked me to take him to the only bar/pub in town. Monte was with me. He was six years old now. We went into the pub with my dad at his request. I was extremely uncomfortable with the atmosphere and hurt that this was where my dad wanted to be on his birthday. Then I turned around and to my horror, sitting in a booth just behind us, was Fred. The old man that had raped me over and over in my teens.

My dad was already stupid drunk and I was already disappointed. Figuring I had no more to lose I got up and went over to Fred and told him I needed to talk to him. He followed me outside to my van where I secured Monte in his car seat before starting a conversation with Fred. The conversation, as far as I was concerned, was going to be my opportunity to confront my abuser. I can't remember every word I said, but I conveyed to him how much what he had done to me had damaged me in ways that would follow me around the rest of my life. He didn't seem to fully understand. He continued to make excuses, the main one being that he had loved me! He semi-quasi apologized for whatever it was that I thought he had done to me, and I could tell he would never understand my position. I decided that it was just going to have to be enough for me that, unlike the majority of rape victims, I at least had the opportunity to face my perpetrator on my terms.

Any feelings of strength I might've gotten from that were quickly blown away when we re-entered the pub. I took Monte back in and slid into the booth with my dad to tell him I was leaving. He asked me what happened outside and I just told him I had confronted Fred. Then before I knew what was happening my dad was buying Fred a beer! Seems he interpreted from my action that I had forgiven the pervert, which I promise you I had not. This hurt me so bad that I quickly left with Monte. And then once outside again I ran right into my ex-stepdad Wade who was entering the bar. *Jesus Christ,* I thought, *is this the gathering place for every man that has ever hurt me?* Then I drove back to Asheville to relate to the magician what I had just gone through.

The magician was disgusted and angry with my dad and so was I. A few nights later, while we were at a hotel in Asheville, I had a very disturbing dream. In the dream I was a little girl of about three or four years old. I could see myself lying on the bed (my old bed in my old room from childhood). My dad and an unrecognizable friend of his entered my room. My dad raped me, as my little child eyes went dead and cold. When I startled awake from this "dream," I was extremely shaken. It felt like a real experience to such a point that I ran into the bathroom and got into the shower. Monte and the magician were still asleep. I let the shower fill the bathtub, then I just lay in the water and cried. The magician must have heard my sobs because before too long he was at the bathroom door wanting to know what had happened. I wasn't sure myself. It felt like I had just experienced some sort of actual memory via a dream and yet I knew I couldn't actually claim to remember this abuse, if in fact it were real. The magician and I talked about it, about how there would always be the possibility of it considering what kind of person my dad was. However, we also discussed the possibility that the rape I had experienced as a teenager at the hands of Fred, a man old enough to be my father, could be crossing over in my subconscious brain. Perhaps it was symbolic of feeling that by way of abandoning me and not protecting me from rape, my dad was responsible in a way. Either way, it was sick and I just wanted to forget it, but it stayed in my head for a long, long, while.

It wasn't long after that, one night when I was back in Tennessee, that my dad called me at home at like 2 a.m. Waking me from my sleep, he was at some bar and had drunk dialed me. I can't remember what he was saying because I was half-asleep and frankly didn't care. I told him that this was unacceptable and that I would not subject Monte to him anymore, conveying that while as a child I had no choice but to be in his presence, going through constant hell and trauma, his grandchild would not! The next day I called the magician to tell him about it and he offered to call my dad and tell him something more. Something that I had not been able to do. I gave him the go ahead and he called my dad and told him to never, ever, call me again at that time of morning, or anytime if he couldn't do any better than that. I heard through the grapevine of my aunt and grandma that my dad was angry as hell to have been called out and down by the likes of a little handicapped man. By "the likes," I mean someone that he considered weaker than himself, at least physically speaking. However, strength is not just a physical measurement and the magician was and always will be one of the strongest people I ever knew. I would not see or speak to my dad again for over a year.

One of my fondest memories of Monte, the magician and I happened during the summer of our last year together. A magic convention was taking place in Orlando, FL, and on the way to it, we stopped in Jacksonville because the magician had bought tickets for Cyndi Lauper in concert. My childhood savior, my favorite singer, my human idol! What made it truly special though was that little Monte was there, six years old, in his little wheelchair. During the concert Cyndi noticed him and after the concert was over she had one of her people come get us. Turns out she wanted to meet Monte! Backstage, when she came around the corner I burst into tears and she hugged me, but then went straight over to Monte and knelt down and had a fifteen-minute conversation with him. Nothing could have been more beautiful.

It was nice to travel around with my two favorite people in the world, keeping busy, laughing a lot, having fun, but I knew it couldn't last, because Monte was going to have to start public school that year. I had been putting off having to make any major life decisions. I was fast becoming exhausted from so much driving between states, taking care of two handicapped people whenever we were on the road, late-night performances, and no real source of stable personal income. I realized I was going to have to slow down enough to do what was best for Monte. What I wanted didn't much matter, because I wasn't even sure about what I wanted, other than for Monte's and my life to be as stable and safe as possible.

I don't think the magician ever took time to try and understand my position. He was too in love with me, and unable to accept that my love for him had limits. He was my guru, my best friend, my direct human link (possibly) to God Himself. I would've done anything for him, for the rest of my life, except be his romantic/sexual lover. In the end, the one thing I could not be was the only thing he wanted and so, reaching an impasse, we said goodbye for the last time.

As Monte grew into school age and the magic shows and travel were behind us, he developed an intense affinity for superheroes. I was glad; it seemed to take the "dark man" out of his mind. From Spiderman to Batman to eventually Venom and The Punisher, Monte developed a fascination for the antihero/

vigilante. He made up superheroes of his own and stories to go along with them. By the time he was ten years old he must have had a hundred or more such characters that he created from his imagination. The running theme for almost every story was justice for the victim. Monte hated criminals and in his stories none of them ever made it out! I suppose he was healing and dealing through creativity.

The Difference

Laughter in the place of frustration
Joy in the place of tears
No worries, no aggravation
The sweetest peace there's been in years
Love in the place of pain
A smile to uplift the frowns
The chance to truly live again
With God's love, clearly all around
No broken bones, or bruises
No broken glass, or shattered hearts
No one hundred mile per hour cruises
No lies, or secrets to tear apart
The biggest difference in today
Is it sees a bright tomorrow
Unlike those saddened yesterdays
There is no pain and sorrow

CHAPTER 11

Settling for, Settling in, but Never Settling Down

I NEVER WANTED TO BE married again. I didn't want to be married the first time. What I wanted was a quiet, safe, nonviolent environment for myself to rest in, and Monte to grow up in. I know it sounds cynical, but love between a man and a woman was not something I believed in. At best, most relationships are held together by a multitude of things that are not love: convenience, common interests, lust, desperation, one person's self-esteem being so low they just settle, fear of being alone/lonely, fear of trying to leave if one party is crazy, financial reasons, for the children—the list goes on and on, and rarely ever comes down to real love.

My Tennessee boyfriend was a hard worker who went to his job every day, even sick. He did not have a violent bone in his body. He was good with children, because he was childlike. He had never been in trouble with the law, or committed any crimes. He did not drink or smoke. He did not own or brandish guns, and most importantly, he was infatuated with me to such a degree he called it love. He was not an attractive man, but he was nurturing and at that point, like an abused dog, if someone was willing to rescue me, feed me and care for me, I was going to stay. I lied to myself a lot to try and make it work, eventually married him and managed for a long while.

For eleven years to be exact. Monte grew, went to school, made friends, had sleepovers, had birthday parties; on holidays we would have big home-cooked meals and invite my mom, sister and her husband. We had a cat. We had a home. We had transportation. We had food. However, one thing I did not have was my health. Seems posttraumatic stress disorder is not just for military men. The term was thrown around every time a doctor couldn't find physical causes for my multitude of ailments. Those ailments were as follows: anxiety, depression, panic attacks, fibromyalgia, TMJ, interstitial cystitis, irritable bowel syndrome, premature ventricular contractions of the heart, premenstrual dysphoric syndrome, endometriosis, reflux, chronic episodes of bronchitis, immune deficiency and eventually pneumonia. My immune system and even my heart, though not "diseased," were damaged, literally and medically. My cardiologist explained it thus: "Your adrenal glands are shot and shrunken; they got stuck on fight or flight and they broke there." Which meant I would be on a beta-blocker for the rest of my life, despite the fact I had no actual heart disease.

The commonality of almost every one of the diagnoses I got was that they were all chronic, syndrome-like ailments that doctors don't have a lot of answers for. They are often overlooked at first because they don't show up in the blood or urine like diseases do. Rather than have tests that accurately diagnose them, it is most often by the process of elimination of other life-threatening illnesses that one gets left with a crapshoot of ailments called syndromes. Since the causes are not tangible (in the blood or urine), there are no "cures." Even though each ailment brings with it a multitude of physical, painful horrors, they are often treated more like emotional illness, from the standpoint that chronic traumatic stress seems to be the originator and perpetuator of each ailment. Therefore, medications used to treat most of them are masks for the symptoms, with no real answers.

Health insurance was my best friend, in that the doctor visits, treatments and medications were constant throughout those eleven years. I was broken, like Humpty Dumpty, and wasn't sure I'd ever be put together again. Despite all this, I did push on with two major areas of my life where I felt led by a higher power to go. One was to work, as a personal fitness trainer. When Monte started his first year of public school, I went back to school too. I found an online college with a Fitness and Nutrition diploma program, that at its end would provide the American Council on Exercise's textbook of study for Personal Trainers. To become ACE certified I would have to pass a rigorous exam, administered only in select big cities. If I failed, it would be a year before I could take the exam again. I studied that manual for six solid months before I even dared. The exam was given in Atlanta, GA and lasted three hours. Once I completed it, I went into the bathroom and cried! I would have to wait two weeks for the test score results to come via regular mail.

It may seem ironic that as my own personal health was breaking down the most, that I would push myself into a profession so physically demanding, but that's just how I am. I push myself, and judge myself way harder than anyone else could ever hope to. The way I figured it, I was a poster child for working out even with health problems and disabilities. If I couldn't cure myself, I could at least inspire others through my work to keep active. It was gloves off as far as I was concerned; nothing was ever going to keep me down again!

This worked out well, because the population I drew to me was often the elderly. Conversations with the elderly are often more meaningful and interesting than the surface bullshit talk that people carry on with day in and day out. Also, the elderly are often suffering from one condition or another, and my own bad health caused an empathy that pretty much carved out a niche for me as a trainer. At the beginning of my job I had days that I would walk in, go straight to the bathroom and cry. I still suffered anxiety whenever I felt trapped, and being committed to even a six-hour shift, knowing that I had no choice but to be there, no matter how uncomfortable I might be, was paralyzing at times. For once though, it mattered enough to work through. This was not some dead-end job, this was a profession, and I told myself that like a mantra. After a couple months or so, I could walk into work freely, without a panic attack.

The second thing that I was supposed to accomplish was much greater, and much scarier than starting and keeping a job. To fully understand how the notion ever crept into my being, or just how divine the guidance for this decision was, I must tell this part in detail. I was on a treadmill, doing my own daily dose of exercise. I had picked up a *Time* magazine to distract me from the agony that was the treadmill. There was an article in there about what China does with many of the baby girls born there. They simply discard them. Put them in the trash or, according to this article, just leave them in drainage ditches. I started to cry, right there on the treadmill. *How awful*, I thought. I regained my composure, finished my workout and stopped by the grocery store to pick up a few things. In the store, the inner voice that communicates directly and personally with me (you can call it my inner consciousness if that's more comfortable. I personally think that it's God, mostly because it's smarter, wiser and less judgmental than my own voice and thoughts) suddenly and out of the blue, loud and resonating, proclaimed: "You will adopt, and it will be like that." That's the other thing about the inner voice that sometimes frustrates me: it is vague, and won't always give me the details, supposedly because working those out is my job! The problem with God throwing me the ball is I often run downfield with it, before waiting for proper instructions. So, of course I took it literally. I'm going to adopt a Chinese baby girl? How? I had not married my boyfriend yet. I was not independently financially capable. I wasn't altogether prepared for such a thing. Still, the inner voice just repeated the same thing: "You will adopt, and it will be like that." Like that? What did that mean?

I told my boyfriend, and he thought it was a wonderful idea. We began looking online at what it would take to adopt a baby girl from China. Right away my worst fears were confirmed. You had to be married, make a certain amount financially, all sorts of roadblocks you couldn't imagine. *Well God, I tried,* I thought, and shut the computer off. Now let me jump around a little, because this adoption theme runs on awhile before any type of "fruition," but we will come back to it.

One night I'm driving home from work. Seventeen miles of long, twisty, back road requires radio to alleviate boredom and I'm jamming to music when about halfway home the inner voice spoke on a different matter. Out of the blue, on a subject I hadn't given thought to in the year since I made up my mind that my dad wasn't fit to be a part of his grandson's life, God asked, "So, could you ever see a way to forgiving your dad?" It threw me off to such a point I cut the radio off. *What?*

Inner dialogue: "Just wondering if there was any way you might see to forgiving him?" *Uh, no!* I cut the radio back on and a couple of minutes go by. Inner dialogue: "Under any circumstance imaginable, might you see your way to forgiving him?" (Cut the radio back off) *Why are you doing this to me? I'm happy right now. I don't want to talk about my dad. I don't want to think about my dad. Would you just drop it!* For the rest of the ride home, no more inner dialogue.

Once I got home however, my boyfriend told me that my aunt had called needing to talk to me, and that it was urgent. I thought *Oh no, what does she want?*, but I called her back. She told me my dad was in the ICU; he had been shot multiple times (nine to twelve, they weren't even sure how many). Seems the crazy, alcoholic and drug-addled woman he had been seeing and recently broken up with, didn't want to break up. So, during an argument she just pulled a .22 rifle out from behind her car seat and started shooting! After hanging up, I didn't know exactly how to feel, but one thing was for certain, this must have been why God was hounding me about my dad. Had God tried to forewarn or prepare me? No matter what you believe personally, you have to admit that's a pretty spooky coincidence.

I drove to North Carolina and went up to the ICU. I walked in to my dad's room. It was horrendous. The visual was the most upsetting thing I had seen since the neonatal ICU Monte had been in. There lay my dad, tubes coming out of his nose draining what looked like thick mucus. Tubes in his torso draining both feces and urine into bags. His body was covered in bloody gauze. Oddly, he was awake, and in a hoarse, whispering voice looked at me and asked, "Do you love me?" I hesitated, maybe two or three seconds, before stammering, "Yeah, yes, of course." His eyes dropped as he said in a hoarse whisper, "You hesitated."

At that moment, I did what I always did in those situations. I made all my own feelings irrelevant and became whatever I needed to be. I approached his side, assured him I loved him, fed him ice chips and watched him slip into an unconscious state. That was the last time he spoke for almost a month. There is a long version and a short version to explain what had happened. The short version is: My dad had lived by the gun, and now looked as if he would die by the gun. The longer version is he and his then girlfriend were both alcoholics. He as usual was violent, mean and cruel. She was on prescription drugs along with alcohol and though I had only met her once she seemed to also be possibly missing a mental component of some sort. When he had broken up with her she had stalked him, broken into his apartment and followed him around town. He had gone to the police but the police didn't really care, given who he was, and so nothing was done about it. Then one night right in front of his apartment as he turned to walk away from her and the argument they were having, she reached in her car and pulled out that .22 and just started shooting him repeatedly in the back. She then covered him with a tarp and left him there to die in the yard. When the paramedics showed up, they had to do an emergency tracheotomy right there on the ground so he wouldn't die from choking on his own blood. He was transported to emergency surgery where nine of the twelve bullets were removed; the others were lodged in places they would just have to stay. His liver was lacerated. His colon was perforated and T9 of the spine was severed. He would be paraplegic for the rest of his life, if he lived.

Amazingly, he did, and after about three months in the hospital, went to a rehabilitation facility for a year. I visited regularly, at least once a month. He was changed forever, and I wondered if that would be for better or for worse. It seemed it was for better, at least emotionally and spiritually speaking. Physically he would suffer and live out his karma in a body that would never allow him to be an alcoholic again. With a bag for a bladder and another bag for a bowel, it was out of the question. It was while he was in this condition that I brought up the adoption story to him. Mostly because I still thought it was literal and that if it ever happened I would have a baby girl of a different race. I wanted to hear what he had to say about that. He said, "Jvonne, I have so many things I have to think about now. Race will never be one of those things I think of again. I have discriminated against minorities my whole life and now, I am one." Ironically, the one-time district attorney who had hated my dad so bad that he saw fit to at least send me to prison was now a private practice attorney. He quickly became defense for the woman who had shot my dad. In the end, she only got six years in prison.

Life went on for some time, about a year and a half before adoption would come up again. In that space of time, I had married my boyfriend, mostly because he wouldn't stop asking. My dad got out of the rehab center and started living with a woman from his past who was willing to try and care for him in that condition. She had a teenage daughter whose best friend had gotten pregnant while on birth control. The pregnant girl already had a two-year-old son and was all set to have an abortion when they told her about my and my husband's wish to adopt. She waited to meet us and decided to go with the adoption option rather than abort. I was elated. God had been right. It was going to happen. So, I guess "it will be like that" meant nothing, because she was white; there was no Chinese baby girl.

We went to all the appointments with her to get ultrasound pictures of the baby. I had contacted a lawyer in Tennessee, who told me because the baby was in North Carolina I would need to get an attorney there for the adoption. Then one night about six months in, I got a call from the girl. She had a brother who had been in Kuwait and he had been killed by a bomb. Between that and her mother's urging, she had decided to keep her baby. I thought I would never stop crying. In fact, I went about in a state of self-pity for a good month. Sometimes I would be driving home and start thinking about the baby that would never be mine and cry until snot poured. It was on one such occasion of crying and self-pitying that the inner voice spoke again.

Inner voice: "Your heart feels ripped out right now doesn't it?" *Yeah, no thanks to You and the lie You told me, that I would adopt.* Inner voice: "So, what if she had given you her baby? Maybe she would then have spent her whole life crying and hurting, just like this." That got my attention, enough to stop crying. I had not thought of it that way. The inner voice continued: "I'm sorry for any misunderstanding, but that wasn't the baby you were sup-posed to adopt, but it is a baby whose life you did save." (Sniff, sniff) *I did?* Inner dialogue: "Yeah, you did. You said you wanted a baby, and it kept her from killing one, and even greater, it gave her time to accept the circumstances and keep her own child." *Wow, I did.* So, I stopped feeling sorry for myself, but I had been burned, and as far as I was concerned I was done trying to figure out what God wanted from me with all this adoption nonsense!

Tigger Shoes and Orange Cheetos

His shining little eyes, his sweet and charming smile
I feel blessed every day that God gave me this child
His hair is fine and curly, his skin is mocha brown
I'm wrapped around the finger, of this precious love I've found
He dances to cartoon music, makes mountains out of clothes
Draws rainbows on my walls, and hits his brother in the nose
His energy is endless, as he runs, and jumps, and plays
Sometimes he drives me crazy, with his little boy ways
He loves to play with hot-wheels, and drive them in my hair
Jump on me while I'm sleeping, but Mommy doesn't care
When you catch this angel sleeping, you would never even know
Most days are crazed with activity, Tigger shoes, and orange Cheetos

CHAPTER 12

Brown Babies

I HAD FORGOTTEN THAT ABOUT a year before, my husband and I had signed up for foster parent training classes as an option for finding the child we were supposed to adopt. Paperwork came in the mail that a round of classes were starting. I felt like throwing them in the trash. I wasn't sure that I could take any more scenarios that involved babies being ripped from my grasp. My husband convinced me that we should at least take the classes while they were being offered. The classes were sponsored by the local Department of Children's Services. We found out they remove a child a day from improper homes in the county where we live. Foster parents were in low supply, but high demand.

Fourteen weeks of PATH training (Parents as Teachers and Healers), which included background checks, fingerprinting, credit checks, etc. We completed the course and were approved as foster parents. Now, we would be called if needed. We had put down certain criteria, because I had Monte's safety to think of; we were only willing to take children eight years old or younger. Monte was ten at the time. Our preferred criteria did not stop

Children's Services from calling one night begging us to take a seventeen-year-old male; we had to decline. Then a few days later we got home to find a request on our answering machine to foster two siblings of two years old and nine months respectively. Although two had never been the plan, we figured we could at least foster them until they were placed somewhere permanently. However, when we called back they had already been placed. Thank God.

Why thank God? Just a week or so later, there was a third phone call, also left on our answering machine. It was a newborn baby! We had been told that babies *never* happened, and even if they did by some miracle, hardly ever did that turn into adoption, because reunification with the baby's family is Children's Service's top priority. I tried all night to call back about this baby but to no avail. The next morning I had to be to work by 6 a.m. and I called every thirty minutes until someone came into the office. I figured, given my luck, this baby would have already been placed too.

As it turned out he was still in the hospital. He had been taken from his mother at birth and put into the custody of the Department of Children's Services. He was biracial—white mom, black dad. I recalled God's words "You will adopt and it will be like that." "Like that" simply meant a baby of a different race. I had never been more sure of anything. My husband and I walked into the nursery of that hospital and looked upon the most beautiful creature I had ever seen, besides my son Monte. This tiny, six-pound, dark-haired, brown baby lay there in a bassinet and I was his mother instantly. I grabbed him, held him to me, fed him his bottle, rocked him, and on the third day, took him home. Although there was a room prepared already, I couldn't bear for him to be anywhere but beside me, or even in the bed, lying on my stomach.

For eleven months, we were his foster parents before we ever got to adopt him. Mostly because, as I mentioned earlier, reunification is the first step they try. If the mother had truly wanted him and had somehow managed to meet Children's Service's criteria for getting him back I would have been devastated. She did make one visit with him at the Department. I saw her, but she had no idea I was the foster parent. She was as blonde and blue eyed as me, a little taller, and very skinny. It is my understanding that although she held him that day, her mother had to keep encouraging her to make eye contact with him, but she really didn't, or couldn't. She was never able to see him again because she failed the first test required of her by the Department, and she never made another attempt. There were other obstacles however that had to be resolved completely before the adoption could be completed. For one, it turned out she was married to a white man, with whom she had two other kids who had been taken away. This white man was the legal father of this baby, even though not the biological one.

Her white husband had no objection to signing away his parental rights and he demanded his wife, the biological mother, sign away her rights as well. I just wanted them both to hurry up and go away. Within the first four months they had both willingly terminated their parental rights. However, the black father was hiding from Children's Services, not wanting to be identified as the father because he thought they were trying to pin him down for child support, when in fact all they wanted was for him to give up his paternal rights. Our caseworker even went so far as to put herself in danger to go to a party she had word he would be attending. She thought maybe that way she could get him to sign the paperwork that would free us up to adopt this precious baby. However, he slipped out the back door and months passed.

Then one night around midnight our home phone rang. I had been sitting up in a chair reading, in between thinking about how this adoption was at a stalemate. Usually, I would have been in bed by ten. I picked up the phone; it was our caseworker. She said, "I have some, uh, goo . . . I have some, I have some news." I sat upright, startled at the late hour she was calling. How could this be good, although, didn't she almost start to say it was good news? What she said next made the hairs on my arms stand up and goose bumps spread over my flesh. The biological father had just been killed in a motorcycle crash. How does one react to such news? Yay? Yikes? In the end, you can only be truthful and admit that you know it is good news. Now a little boy can have a family that has loved him from first sight . . . no . . . loved him since God said he would be . . . which was before he was ever even born.

They took DNA from the father's body postmortem, and I took the baby to a clinic where they swabbed for DNA, and it was 99.9 percent sure that the deceased was the biological father. Now, his parental rights were gone with his body. On November 11, 2005, just a few days shy of his first birthday, that little brown baby became legally ours. Finally, I could give him his name rather than just call him "sweet baby, precious, sweet angel, beautiful baby, sweet boy" . . . I had it bad for this baby, what can I say!

I wish I could say that we all lived happily ever after, but how often is that how life goes? Developmental delays in speech/language were the first hurdles this little boy encountered, followed by a hyperactivity that gave him the strength and energy of a raging bull. Attention deficit so bad that he wouldn't sit still for me to read the simplest children's books to him. He was a happy and loving child but if you told him no, or something upset him, he would run head first into solid walls, then throw himself backwards onto concrete floors. The thing is, until a child reaches a certain testable age there is no diagnosis given, nor treatment available. There were times I would sit in the closet and cry thinking if he didn't get meds I was going to need some! The worst part wasn't my little boy though, because he couldn't help what he was going through. The real reveal here was that I was truly alone in trying to do what was best for his optimal well-being. I was alone in a lot of things. The addition of this child to our family really highlighted that for me.

Monte had always been a breeze to parent. He might have been physically handicapped, but he was the perfect child from the standpoint of being respectful, easy to get along with and literally never requiring much in the way of discipline. He and I were such kindred spirits that it had never occurred to me that I was parenting him alone, but I was. Only now, with a child of a much different temperament, did I fully see that my husband and I were not on the same page at all. It seemed he was too concerned with being the favorite parent, and often let things happen that were detrimental, in my opinion. Like not being able to say no to any request our little boy had. Example: At age one and a half the poor child pretty much potty trained all over the home carpets, because my husband would give him as many cups of apple juice as he requested. A sixty-four-ounce empty container later was pure diarrhea. In the beginning, it was incidents like that, but the pattern was becoming clear. Our baby had issues with impulse control and at least one parent was not providing acceptable boundaries.

Not only that, but with a new addition to the family I got an incredible view of how much I did without adequate support. I managed the finances, tried to keep the house clean, worked a job outside the home and took the children to their doctor and therapy appointments. I had my own health problems to deal with. On top of that, my husband had some sort of online porno addiction that I was tired of discovering, fighting about, and never understanding. He also spent money like a teenager with no family responsibilities, and no matter how many times I tried to manage, consolidate and get us out of debt he would just pile on more credit card expenses until we were drowning! I had no idea just how unhappy I was until I wrote a poem that I shared with a friend at the gym, who after reading it asked, "Are you going through a divorce?" I remember thinking *Wow, I wish!*

On top of all this, the rest of my family just piled on. My sister, her husband, and my mom, all living together just a half-mile from our house, kept the trail from their house to mine hot with complaints and whining about their respective lives. They were asking for advice, needing to borrow money, crying over each other's actions, complaining about life in general. My dad was living with his sister now, because the woman he had been living with was an alcoholic who ended up dropping him on the floor and breaking his femur bone. Shortly thereafter he had to have one of his legs amputated from the knee down. While he was in the hospital for that I had gone to visit him. He had a terrible bedsore they were fighting to keep infection out of. When the nurse who was caring for him came into the room I had myself a little shiver.

It was the girl from the drugstore fight-turned-stabbing all those years ago. I followed her into the hallway and asked her if she remembered me. She played a little game of pretending not to at first but then I guess it surprised her that my next words were an apology. For one thing, I didn't want her recognition of me to affect the care she needed to give to my dad. For another, despite who started it, whose fault it had been, or any other extenuating circumstances, I wanted to be bigger and better than that and own my part. She made some offhand comment about how we all do crazy things and how she herself had things from her past she regretted. Then she walked away.

As soon as school was out that summer of 2009, I put my two boys in the car and drove hundreds of miles away to a beach in Florida with no husband, no mom, no sister, no dad, no job, no anything. I felt like if I didn't get away from everybody but my kids, I might end up in a mental hospital. Words cannot begin to describe how at the end of my rope with my current life I felt. I spent the whole summer away, thinking, breathing, contemplating, and clearing my head of all the clingy, needy voices that had cluttered it for so long. I also discovered yoga that summer, something that I would eventually start teaching as part of fitness programming.

When we got back home after that summer break I got a divorce and chose to legally become a single parent, which is what I felt like anyway, even during the marriage. I had, mostly out of responsibility to my children, stayed married three years longer than I should have. If I had displayed the courage to accept my own truth rather than try to manufacture the one that would keep everybody else happy, I would have been divorced already. I realized post-divorce that I hadn't been in love with my husband like one is supposed to love a spouse. I had cared for him like a child; I felt pity, empathy, responsibility, sadness and worry for him, but not love like you should have for your husband and life partner. He had made me feel responsible for his happiness by using passive-aggressive behaviors that included guilting and displaying massive lack of self-esteem. I was so disappointed to find yet again that my children aside, real love just didn't seem to exist or be in the cards for me.

The next year Monte entered high school. It was a huge change. He had gone to only one school first through eighth grade and had the same classmates all those years. Now everyone was dispersing between three different high schools. In the end, only a handful of his classmates from his childhood school ended up at the same high school with him. By his own admission, he was lonely and introverted that entire ninth grade year. He wore a hooded coat every day, even when it was hot. He said he just wanted to disappear into the background and hope no one noticed. It was hard for him to socialize or get into the new environment of high school. One reason was that mostly all the clubs were either physically demanding sports-type stuff or just didn't interest him. He had a wonderful reading teacher though and he talked about her a lot in a positive way.

One night I lay awake pondering all this when it hit me like a ton of bricks: Comic Book Club! What if Monte could start a new club at his school, one where both aspiring artists and writers could come together and share ideas and create those ideas into something. When I shared this idea with Monte I saw the light shine once more in his eyes. He was excited and brought the prospect up to his reading teacher. She helped him get the dream realized by agreeing to be the school staff member overseeing the club. As it turned out though, they wanted me to plan, lead and oversee the activities and content.

The next year Monte's high school got a new club, Comic Book Club. On Club Day, when interest meetings for all clubs are held, we got eighty-six people signed up. The largest turnout ever for a school club at Monte's high school. Unlike other clubs that just met once a month during school on Club Day, we had after-school meetings every week. Despite the eighty-six-person roster, only about fifteen of the most serious showed up week after week for the after-school meetings. When we started, I wasn't even sure what exactly we were all about, but it didn't take long to figure it out.

Monte used both his creative talents and his empathetic heart to develop a club motto and creed: "Comic Book Club, where you can create superheroes or you can be one." Being one meant volunteer work. Monte wanted to use his club as a way of reaching out to the community through volunteer work. I must say as those three years of club and Monte's high school career flew by, I learned as much as anybody there. For one, what it meant to be not only accepted but revered for being myself. Sure, it was by a group of nerdy teenagers, but I found it very healing on the inside, where my own school days and peers had left me wounded.

We volunteered at nursing homes, the local children's hospital, for the local recycling initiative, any and all 5K foot races for a plethora of causes, and even hospice. These kids impressed me with their dedication and enthusiasm. It was more than a club by senior year. It was a freaky little side family that stuck together and accomplished much. Monte graduated in 2014, cap and gown procession, attainment of the diploma, and even scholarship to a two-year college. My heart felt like a helium balloon, rising to the sky, ready to burst with pride and happiness. This boy with a bearded face was a man now. He had, despite his physical handicap, made it beyond where I had been at his age, and nothing could have made me prouder.

I had pushed on single in my day-to-day life for those three years, while I dated a man that to this day is my best friend. It was nice because it was the first time in my life that I had ever dated! All my relationships with men before had been either pushed on me, long term and chaotic, or overlapping, which is just damn weird. I had not been free of the 24/7 presence of a man since the age of fifteen! Now here I was, forty years old and finally going to get the opportunity to fall in love naturally and normally? I was scared for a lot of reasons. What if I was too damaged for this man? I mean he came from a good family. A stable family. I met his father and he was a righteous and upstanding man. My goodness! Two of them? Righteous men I mean. What kind of parallel universe had I fallen into? What if he hurt me just like all the others?

Luckily the Universe kept my heart open to love even as I doubted human nature. I soon discovered that if you start a relationship with mutual respect, genuine honesty and a shared sense of humor there is nothing you can't share or become to each other. I had never experienced that level of intimacy with anyone. Apparently, God saved the best for last and I am eternally grateful. I was blessed to finally meet the man that God had made for me. I suppose I could piss and moan about it taking so long, or all those years wasted on empty versions of the real thing. Rather, I realize that he came at just the right time. He missed the crazy, the dysfunctional, the angry, the ugly, the violence, the horror and the hell. Thank God! He got here just in time for the healing, the strengthening, the peace seeking, the laughter, and the beauty that is unconditional love.

I walk a fine line every day of my life, seeking balance and harmony in my actions, speech and deeds. I am imperfect, and so this is why it is a daily practice, rather than a one time and done deal. Love helps! Everyone wants to be loved and cared for. Those that are, sometimes take it for granted, and those that are not, often act out in vile ways from never having had it. I don't believe in having regrets about life because that indicates that you believe you have somehow failed at it. I believe, in spite of the horrors, the trials and the tribulations, to change even one small thing out of regret could change the entire course of your life and rob you of the things that do in fact make you happy. For these reasons, I wouldn't change anything, for it is my journey, as it has been, that got me to this point. However, if I had been given just one finely honed super power to take with me through life it would have been *self*-honesty!

Sometimes it feels like I am a hundred years old, for all the life I've lived, for all the times I've persevered in search of a better and happier existence. I have been given an opportunity to rest easy for the first time in my life, and in that environment I am healing every day from the treacheries of my past. I am not worried about my future either. These moments will become part of my past as well and eventually I will have so many beautiful memories that there will be no room for the old, ugly ones.

I fall deeper in love with my life partner each passing day. His love is so complete that I finally know what it feels like to feel safe, secure, and stable. Basking in the basic foundations of consistent love, I hope for a lifetime of togetherness. However, I will never hold another human being to the impossible task of ensuring my happiness.

The Monster

I've been trying to contain the monster,
but that was the wrong approach
You have to make friends with your
own sins and move forward with faith and hope
I've been trying to find the monster
I want to know where he lives
Sometimes he lies, but deep in his eyes
I know he wants me to forgive
I've been trying to kill the monster,
but nothing I throw at him stops him
He pushes on, never leaves me alone
and wants me to eventually love him
I've been trying to know the monster
I swear he sounds a lot like me
But then it was him, who started my sin
Then abandoned and forsaken me
I've tried to bury the monster,
but I swear that he still lives
Beyond the grave, in my head, in my name
Just a phantom of what he couldn't give
I've been trying to tame the monster,
but he's too wild to tame
So, I put him to rest, then I did my best
To let my light shine through all the pain

CHAPTER 13

The Darkness Dies

WHEN I STARTED WRITING THIS book, which was many, many times, for many years in terms of starting in any real way, always I wondered *how do you end a life story, when the life isn't over yet?* I was stuck mulling this over when my "Ole Grandmother Hubbard" passed away in July of 2015. I loved my Grandma Hubbard; she was a simple woman who had a hard life, but a long one. She was ninety when she left this world. I didn't go to the funeral. No one understood that and it hurt some feelings, I'm sure. My dad was hurt more than anyone because I did not go to support him. I didn't go because I knew how it would go . . . guilt-ridden relatives crying and carrying on, talk of death like death itself was redemption, talk of God and how not to know Him was spiritual death, and finally relatives fighting about who might get what. The one thing that wouldn't be told was the truth.

The truth was my aunt talked to her aging mother like she was a dog. One cousin's behavior had made my grandma cry so many times we had all lost count. The aunt and cousin were of the temperament and disposition that I knew they would be wailing like life was over for them. They had so much guilt that they would cry for themselves, not Grandma. Then there was my dad, whose guilt would probably be the greatest. In the heyday of his partying, KKK, alcoholic, criminal ways he had caused our whole family to have to give up their family land. After my parents' divorce, my dad sold out the property my grandparents had given him to a developer, who then pressured my grandparents and uncle into subsequently selling theirs.

As I contemplated my position I envisioned myself unable to hold my tongue. I did not want to dishonor my grandma by punching her daughter or other granddaughter in the face when they started up. Nor did I feel like going to jail ever again, and since I couldn't see any way to keeping my mouth shut I stayed at home. However, I did "sad text" my dad, a few days after Grandma died. I'll never really know why I did it, but I lit into him about all the pain he had caused Grandma back in the day. Did I still resent him that much? Maybe. Did the Universe want him to hurt some more? Who knows? What I did know was that I was starting to feel as if he had outlived my forgiveness. He had survived being shot twelve times—like some sort of fucking miracle—said he was a changed man and did stop drinking. For years, I thought maybe he had changed and maybe he had seen the Light, but the truth is that for over a month before Grandma died I had been disappointed in what I had seen trending on his social media page.

By the time Grandma died, that South Carolina shooting, where a white boy went inside a black church and sat for two hours praying and worshipping with the congregation before opening gunfire upon them had already happened. For almost a month straight, social media and the back corners of pickup trucks everywhere in the South started up with rebel flags! With the force that we should all be using for world peace, these people came out with renewed support of the confederate flag? What this had to do with the actual tragedy of so many lives lost I do not know. All I know is I got really sick of hearing about that damn flag's right to fly instead of anything much about the victims in that church. It shouldn't surprise any reader here that my dad ended up being one of those people. His social media page became nothing but a poster board of rebel flags, KKK photos and such, General Lee memes, Civil War posts, and lots and lots of talk about guns!

Yeah, I found it hurtful. Yes, I took it personally. He had a half-black grandson of nearing social media age; had he not thought of that? Not to mention I thought he was through with all the racial hate and misplaced pride in being the color white. After being shot he had even been pen pals for quite some time with a local black girl accused of murder. Yet here it was every day, something new and disappointing. He started to wonder about why I was distancing myself even further from him, and when I told him how I felt he mailed me two money orders for a thousand dollars each! Which I drove straight to North Carolina to give back to him, as I told him that wasn't how things worked. He had looked ashamed and just shook his head saying, "Jvonne, you're just a different kind of person." He languished on this earth nine more months after Grandma died, then on April 15, 2016, after nearly fifteen years of living out his karma in a broken, sickly, wrecked body he finally surrendered just three days after his sixty-fifth birthday.

The last time I saw him alive I knew it would be the last time. His stumps where legs had once been were both infected to the point of oozing and bleeding. He had become unable to talk above an inaudible whisper and he could not eat. He had me call him an ambulance and follow behind it to the hospital on that last visit. His little brown grandson and I went inside the ER once they had him settled. As my son's eyes filled with tears upon seeing his grandpa's condition, my dad told him to never be ashamed to cry. That was a lot coming from him, who had told me my whole life to *never* let anyone see you cry, lest they know they had hurt you. I didn't cry. I just felt the surrealism of how he would not go out with a bang as expected but rather a whimper.

On his birthday he was still in the hospital, fresh out of ICU from another surgery. All the metal pins and rods that had been placed in the leg that had suffered the femur break had to be cut out and removed because they were pushing through and out his infected stump. It was a mess. I had called to check on his status and the nurse held the phone to his ear because he was too weak to hold it, or even talk really. The only words he uttered were, "Weak . . . too weak to talk," and so I told him I loved him and Happy Birthday. Then I got in the shower and cried heavily as I knew it would be the last time I ever heard his voice. They sent him home the next day, where he lived for two more days without my ever calling to check on him again.

When the call came that he had passed away, I cried for two days straight. There was a heavy, dark, painful cloud that burdened my heart and overwhelmed my soul. Then on the third day, I went to his funeral on Big Hill Cemetery, in Brevard. Pulling up to the scene was like something out of hillbilly heaven—rednecks, ruffians and rebel flag—flying pickup trucks parked in the grass all along the hill. We were actually five minutes late because of my aunt not having her shit together. Then to my dismay I saw a section of the USMC standing by to give him flag status ceremony all because my aunt, whom he had lived with most of the fifteen years since he was shot, had lied to the funeral home that he was a proud marine.

I assure you, he was not. My dad was mostly a coward and a bully (and that's being kind). He went to Camp Lejeune military training camp in 1969, completed basic training then boarded a bus for Camp Pendleton in California where he was to be shipped out to Vietnam. He would have been on the front lines given his proficiency with guns. However, out of fear, anxiety or whatever caused it he got as far as the bus station in California, bought a bus ticket straight back to Brevard and never reported for duty. His boots never touched the ground to defend this country and yet there we sat before his coffin, going through a military ritual that should sacredly be reserved for heroes.

Words were thrown around like *honorable, of service to, bravery for the sake of his countrymen's peace and freedom*. Then two majors folded up the American flag, knelt before my aunt and presented it to her, then they took it back to the funeral home until she could get some sort of paperwork straight. Uh, paperwork? You mean, more like the letter of amnesty signed by

President Carter in 1977 to pardon all Vietnam draft dodgers? As the story I've been told my whole life goes, my mom met my dad in 1971 when he was already AWOL. They started living together, but within a few months he was caught by local police in Hendersonville, North Carolina and sent back to Camp Lejeune to face the prison there called the brig. However, after only two weeks there he escaped the brig by way of a ruse that involved a building the prisoners were constructing on site. He had smuggled in his civilian clothes and a straw hat he had bought from the canteen, and threw them into this incomplete building. Then the next day while working alongside the other prisoners he jumped into that building, changed clothing and of all things hailed a taxi that drove him right out the front gate!

After that he and my mom ran from the FBI constantly, marrying in 1972 and getting pregnant with me in Nashville, Tennessee by late 1973. As they moved cross-country back and forth my pregnant mom was crawling out of second-story windows in the middle of the night and crossing rivers waist deep in the cold of winter. They fled the FBI from North Carolina, South Carolina, Georgia, Tennessee, Boston, even Canada, and back to North Carolina to his parents (my grandpa and grandma Hubbard's house.) My grandma had cut a hole in the floor of her laundry room that would allow him to hide underneath the house. Whenever the FBI came there looking, which they did numerous times, they never suspected that an old worn rug, clutter and laundry baskets were hiding a hole in the floor for him to "Houdini" into whenever they showed up at the front door.

During that entire time on the run he used the birth certificate and social security number of his own little dead brother, who had passed away at seven months old. To this day my birth certificate lists my dad's name as Truman, instead of his real name Joel, because they were still on the lam when I was born in 1974.

Anyway, I sat through the mockery funeral without saying a word, or shedding a tear. I had odd thoughts, like, *If every person standing on this hill who ever donned a KKK robe along with my dad were still in costume, at least twenty people would have been wearing hooded sheets!* I waited until everyone else went away, then, holding up the funeral home staff for a good thirty minutes, I sat by the coffin, with my right hand on it. I read aloud The Great Liberation Through Hearing section of the *Tibetan Book of the Dead*. My hope in so doing? That his soul might move away from any notion of return and hopefully just go back to the Source! He had hurt so many people during his short time on this earth. I didn't think the Universe needed a repeat of Joel Hubbard—style energy.

That black, dark, heavy cloud that caused me to cry for two days was finally lifting. All the sadness had been for the tragedy alone that was his wasted life. For all that wasn't, that never had been and was now never going to be, I had cried. It wasn't so much for him personally; it couldn't have been, because I had been grieving my daddy my *whole* life. By the time his life ended there was nothing left for me to grieve. God had given me a glimpse of how it all ends for a person like that. As I walked away from the coffin I couldn't help but note the irony as two men moved in to lower it into the ground. It was a poignant moment because one of them was a black man and he was the one who picked up the shovel and began throwing the dirt in on top of my dad. In the end, his hate was all for naught. I wish I could say The End right here but there was still one more thing that I felt I needed to do, and when I did it, it opened up the story all over again.

Letting Go

Take off the armor, lay down the blade
Look to the sunshine, you are wonderfully made
You don't have to run now, there is nothing to fear
You've chased down your demons, I love you my dear
Let go of the pain, let go of the rage
Embrace what you've learned, then release it to space
Turn towards the middle, turn towards The Way
Share authentic you, all is well, Namaste

CHAPTER 14

Joel Hubbard's Daughter

HE HAD BEEN A FORCE to be reckoned with and now he was dead. It was bound to have been confusing and emotional for me at best, but "it was never going to be any other way." Those were the only words I could even come up with as I tried to comfort my poor ole uncle. My dad's older brother sat graveside with tears in his eyes. He looked so old and sad. It made me realize just how much my uncle looked like my beloved Grandpa Hubbard, who had been gone for almost thirty years now.

My daddy had been a phantom in my life for most of it. A horrific, violent force who blew through with anger and sadness, destruction and darkness, and affected my life so deeply that I had to write a book about it! It doesn't matter to me what people think about that. The truth, as honestly and genuinely as I could possibly remember it, is finally out. Out of me. I've been embarrassed and ashamed of being a Hubbard for most of my life. Embarrassed that my dad was a racist, embarrassed that my dad was a criminal, a drunk, a low life right up until the very end it seems. I had been ashamed and believing for years that I was tainted with what I saw as the stains upon me. Sins of the father and whatnot, leading to my own dark splotches that I would seek my whole life to nullify by way of the Light.

Still there is a sadness in my heart for this bad man, Joel Hubbard, who I loved so very much for nothing. It was never going to be any other way though, meaning we the family had always known it would end this way. Bloody, empty, hollow and dark. Pain in our hearts and minds for all the times he had hurt us. Sorrow for never understanding how we were supposed to feel anything but cheated. Yet he had possessed a strange magnetism that I still can't explain. I'm not sure that was ever a good thing, because it drew you in and tricked you into loving him no matter what he had done. It certainly was never going to feel fair to be in any relationship with Joel Hubbard, because you were going to be at an immediate disadvantage. So being Joel Hubbard's daughter had never made me happy or proud, but now it was all over, save this one last thing I felt I must do. I had a peace that surpasses understanding come over me, and it was in that vein that I took what was mine and for a moment the world was right and it was okay to be Jvonne Hubbard. Hell, not only was it okay, it was going to require it.

That one more thing I needed to do, for it to feel over and honest, was to call my cousin Kaylee. After all, Kaylee had been the one who supplied my dad his last meal—carrot cake, his favorite. He had managed to eat one piece before dying in his sleep. At the time, I had been grateful for that, because he hadn't eaten anything but IV for over two weeks. Kaylee worked as an aide for my dad, running errands, light housework, etc. It was a position given to her and paid for by the state of North Carolina. I couldn't bear to think she might grieve an uncle who had perhaps betrayed her, so I felt I had to tell her something that I had wanted to tell her for years. Something I thought I had seen once while on a visit to my dad way back in 2008. So, the day after the funeral, I called her cell phone to tell her this bothersome thing that I will share here now, also, with you.

About eight years before, back in 2008 or so, Kaylee had been married with two children. Her husband had an accident at work that herniated discs in his back, which caused him immense pain. So much so that he got addicted to prescription hydrocodone. During this same time frame my dad, (her Uncle Joel) had a state Medicaid—paid for *permanent* prescription of his own for hydrocodone, due to the pain of living inside a body that had been shot twelve times. The thing is that at that particular time, he wasn't in severe pain. In 2008 he had not yet had either of his paralyzed legs amputated. He was proud of not needing to take the hydrocodone.

On this fateful visit back in 2008, the kids and I were about to leave. My aunt that Dad lived with had been on the phone all secret-like with somebody for over ten minutes. Then I saw my cousin Kaylee's husband Bruce pull up out at the barn-like building my dad often spent time in during the day. Everyone knew Bruce had a drug problem. He had gotten addicted to hydrocodone quite quickly. Now his problem was so bad, it was rumored he had stolen from both my grandma and my uncle for drug money. What was he doing out there? Where was Kaylee? I asked these questions of my aunt. She attempted to explain that my dad sometimes felt sorry for Bruce being in so much pain. Something didn't sound right, so I waited until Bruce left, then I walked out to the building to ask Dad for myself what had just happened. His story was the same: he felt sorry for Bruce, being in pain and all, so he sometimes "spared" a few of his hydrocodone. At the time, I remember wondering if I should call Kaylee and tell her, in the end opting not to because stepping into anyone's marital troubles is usually messy. Plus, she had to know what her husband was capable of.

Yet present day, when I revealed all this to my cousin, who these eight years later is a single mom of two boys because she had to divorce her drug-addict husband, she said, "I knew, Jvonne, because Bruce finally admitted it around the time of our divorce." Then she told me the part I didn't know. My dad had never been "sparing" anything. He had however been selling them to Bruce for street value (which can be anywhere from two to three dollars per pill), month after month, for over four or five years. That all told it had cost their family over ten thousand dollars. Not to mention the costs to the marriage, the children and the home that no monetary amount could ever be placed upon. Compounding this already nauseating revelation, my cousin Kaylee said that my uncle (her dad) had gone to my dad and begged him to stop selling drugs to Bruce. My uncle cited how Kaylee's children were going without because of it. My dad's response had been, "They don't look like they're going without to me." His heartless remark, a jibe to the fact that they were big boys.

Then another memory flashed across my mind from that same time period in 2008. In a Bible that he had kept by his bed, my dad had hundreds of hundred dollar bills "saved." He hid them in between glued-together pages inside. He had shown it to me once all those years ago, saying he wanted me to know where it was in case he died and it would pay for his funeral. I don't know why he bothered telling me though, because my aunt whom he lived with also knew and she would undoubtedly get to it first. In my mind, she would have the money in hand before he was cold in the ground!

Dad had told me he was saving every month from his disability check to put that money there for his eventual funeral. All the while it was drug money sacrilegiously glued between the pages of the Bible. Now it was evident that my aunt had paid for that elaborate sham and mockery of a military funeral with the blood, sweat, tears and addiction of my poor cousin's destroyed family. She was the one setting it up by phone for my dad and Kaylee's husband, so as to keep Kaylee in the dark as much as possible.

I excused myself from the phone conversation with Kaylee, telling her I would call her back some other time. My mind was whirling, anger seared my veins, I was disgusted with Joel Hubbard all over again! The worst part of it all was that he had been sober when he committed this atrocity. There was no alcoholic blackout to blame it on. In his supposed "changed man" years, post-paralysis, he had done this. Just then I was overcome by my old friend rage. I walked to the back of my van and retrieved the three items that had belonged to my dad, that I had taken from his room the day of the funeral. A wooden Indian statue, a wooden frame I had given him containing a picture of us when I was a little girl, and a wall clock/safe. One by one I smashed them against a stump in my backyard, as I screamed "your time's up motherfucker!" Afterwards I sat in the dirt laughing and crying at the same time, bleeding from my hand where the glass of the frame had cut it. *Nothing* could make this right, but I was damn sure gonna try! When I calmed down I went inside and made one more phone call.

My aunt's daughter Jessica had been the one who had to make all the funeral arrangements and had taken care of obituary details and such for my dad. My aunt had collapsed in a chair citing the stress and loss, and her inability to deal or cope, as reasons why she couldn't deal with it herself. So, I asked my cousin Jessica just how much the funeral had cost? Not having any reason not to tell me, she freely offered up the information: $6,200. In the telling she said that just within a couple hours of my dad's dead body being removed from the apartment he and my aunt had shared, my aunt had called Jessica to help her with all this. "This" being a search for money that my aunt claimed my dad had hidden somewhere in his room. My aunt produced a small key, but didn't know exactly what it was to, or where Dad had said something was. Cousin Jessica had dug around for two hours in my dad's room postmortem, looking for his funeral money! Frustrated, Jessica had asked my aunt multiple times, "Are you sure you don't know where he would keep it?" To which she had replied things like, "It could be anywhere, in a book, in a magazine, in a box, in a picture frame, in a safe!" After two hours of searching, deep in the back of my dad's closet, Jessica said she finally found a small lockbox safe. She brought it out to my aunt, and the key opened it. Inside was $11,300!

Chills went down my spine! Kaylee's family. Kaylee's marriage and children. Kaylee's money had paid for that military mockery funeral and now there was still $5,100 more in my aunt's possession! As I said this out loud Jessica responded that she doubted very much money was left, because even before my dad was cold in the ground my aunt had spent the night with her and sat writing fifteen to twenty money orders out, for what and to whom, no one knew. I shared with Jessica what her mother and my father had done to our cousin Kaylee and it sickened her as much as it did me. Again, I excused myself from the phone, because now I knew what I had to do.

I spent the next three days raging, planning, not sleeping and staying awake till 3 a.m. Scenarios were flashing through my head at record speed as to what could be done about all this, and how. I did a couple of things from home in Tennessee, like call and email the funeral home in North Carolina to tell them the truth of how they had been lied to, and to request they never relinquish that graveside flag to my aunt, ever! I also called the Brevard Police Department, and spoke with an officer there about the guns my dad had admitted to having in his room prior to his death.

In fact, at my 2015 Christmas visit I had asked my dad how many guns he had, and he had told me eleven. I had asked him at that time to give them to me as an act of full surrender, to a supposed changed man lifestyle. He had been taken aback at the thought, stating guns were his therapy. Then he conceded that I could have them after his death. It's not that I wanted them; I hate guns. I had just wanted to take them out of that environment. Now, the officer told me there was nothing they could do at this point. They had no legitimate reason to even obtain entry to that apartment, with no crime having been committed. I expressed my concern that my aunt might start doling these guns out to other unstable and non-law-abiding members of the family. The officer then asked me if there had been a will. There had not, I told him. "Well then," he said, "you're the daughter and she's just the sister, meaning you are the legal heir of his everything." He suggested I call the clerk of court and perhaps consult an attorney, but I knew that wouldn't fly with the sort of person I was dealing with. In my lifelong experience with her, my aunt had long been a delusional drama queen who had abandoned her mental health counseling sessions years ago. Now she was borderlining on being a pill head. She was a selfish, greedy woman whose narcissism would bleed through anytime she thought she could get something for nothing. I knew if I got an attorney, she would hide or give away everything to avoid doing any semblance of the right thing!

The right thing, however, was what God was compelling me from within to do. So once again I calmed down and listened to that peaceful all-knowing voice, instead of going off half-cocked based on anger and disgust. Once I began to focus, the plan was given to me from within, with permission to carry out as I saw fit, so long as I harmed none. So, I packed my oldest son's Batman book bag with supplies: several of the brass Hindu deities from my worship of the Supreme, *The Tibetan Book of the Dead*, duct tape and rope (just in case) and of course a blade! Then along with the companionship of my son Monte and his good friend Jacob, we headed to North Carolina to spend the weekend (if need be) with my aunt.

When we got there, she was beyond glad to see us, mostly because it was the one-week anniversary of my dad's death. There she was alone in the apartment, alienated from her own daughter because they had argued the night before. No one wanted to stay there with her in the apartment of death and she proclaimed that everyone had abandoned her in her time of need. It was obvious right away that I wouldn't need the duct tape or the rope (thank God); feeding her personality type was going to be all I needed to do!

For the next eight hours as we all sat about the apartment conversing, listening to my aunt bemoan, complain and cry, I made frequent trips to the "bathroom" and "my van" throughout. During these trips to the bathroom and the van I was removing recovered guns, about three hundred or so rounds of ammo, twenty-two knives, eighteen bottles of aging alcohol and a vase of my dad's full of change. Later at the local grocery store I used a money changing machine to turn that change into the mere $96 it was. By nightfall I was frustrated to have not found all the guns or even a drop in the bucket of money!

My aunt finally went to bed around midnight and the boys fell asleep on her living room couches, but I was wide awake. I watched the clock go from 1 a.m. to 2 a.m. to 3 a.m. and exhaustion, both physical and mental, was setting in. My aunt's apartment was stuffy and extremely hot inside, so at 3:30 a.m. I went outside for some air and began to converse with God about how if I didn't get some sleep I didn't know how I could keep this up all weekend! Then it occurred to me . . . *hey there's a king's ransom of alcohol in the floorboard of my van right now; perhaps I'll just have a couple of shots to put me to sleep.* Let me pause here to explain why this wasn't necessarily a good idea. For starters, there's the loom of the alcoholic gene. Beer is nasty, wine is delicious, and hard liquor . . . well, it probably shouldn't be for human consumption, least of all by a 115-pound female.

Besides, I had once sworn to my twenty-one-year-old son that I would never drink again. The past had once produced an ugly accidental drunk that had occurred from ingesting homemade hillbilly cough medicine at my dad's suggestion. After that I had promised my son I would never drink again. Ah, but my human weakness prevailed and I rationalized that I was never going to get to sleep if I didn't drink something. I crawled over the backseat to look upon my choices. As my eyes traveled the row of bottles I remember thinking how unfair it was that they package this poison in beautiful bottles that draw you to them and suck you in. I selected the smallest bottle, not that it mattered considering it was 80 proof. I sat on the porch and poured myself a "shot" in a water glass, and five minutes later I poured myself another "shot," still in a water glass. I only mention the water glass to illustrate that I'm guessing the two "shots" were extremely generous. Then, feeling the warmth creep through me, I went inside and lay down on the bed beside my aunt to hopefully get some sleep. It was 4 a.m. I had no more than snuggled my head into the pillow when something bizarre happened. I'm going to go out on a limb and suggest that what happened was the chemicals in my brain were flooded with alcohol and I was drunk in every sense of the word.

The following gets a bit sketchy for me at times, because contrary to what I had always believed to be an alcoholic lie, uh, you can blackout. Especially if you're throwing up and committing self-injuries, but I get ahead of myself . . . I rolled over onto the top of my aunt and straddled her in her sleep. I leaned down and kissed her right on the mouth. She awoke trying to sit up, but I leaned down again and kissed her forehead and said, "I'm not a lesbian, but I am going to tell you the truth." My aunt looked confused for a moment, then surely smelling the liquor on my breath, asked, "Have you been drinking?" "Yes!" I replied. "Yes I have and now Joel Hubbard is here and he is going to talk to you through me." At this she screamed and threw me off her! I landed on the floor in a crack between the bed and a baby crib of her grandchild's. I struck the left side of my head hard on that crib while going down. Then I started to puke. By this point the boys had heard the ruckus and ran into the room where my aunt was nervously jumping around screaming, "Help her!" Jacob tried to lift me up off the floor, but I fought him and crawled away towards the bathroom. Instead, I accidentally ran my forehead smack into a mirrored headboard that was sitting on the floor. The next thing that happened I don't remember for myself but my son and Jacob say that I then flopped backwards into a five-tier mirrored shelf and cracked the back of my head against it so hard that my eyes rolled back in my head. My eyes then closed and I became still enough that they grabbed up the phone prepared to call an ambulance, even though it would end our ruse.

However, before they could dial 911, I sat bolt upright wide-eyed, projectile vomited again and then crawled successfully into the bathroom begging to be submerged in water. I could hear my aunt anxiously shrieking commands at the boys for them to help me. I don't know why she never bothered to assist. Jacob lifted me up still fully clothed and put me in the bathtub where I would spend the next two hours running cold water over my body and drinking it occasionally, in between multiple counts of vomiting. I was told that during that time I cursed the Hubbard family bloodline all the way back to my grandpa, who had also been an alcoholic.

Anyway, sometime around 7 a.m. I was put to bed finally. I only slept until 8:30 a.m. though, before I awoke fully sober but horribly worse for the wear. I felt ready to just give up on any hope of finding the money or any more guns. I wanted to go home. Just then Jacob came in to check on me. Seeing that I was awake he leaned down to whisper to me that in my drunken stupor and subsequent falling about, my aunt had made the proclamation that there were guns nearby. "Okay," I whispered back. As he went back to the living room where they were all sitting and talking, I could hear my aunt complaining about all the vomit she was going to have to steam clean up from her carpet. As I raised up from the bed to start looking about the cluttered—I dare say hoarder-style—bedroom I found one more gun. Total to that point on guns: seven.

Then I leaned down to temporarily shove the gun under the bed until I could get fully dressed, but a long stream of vomit down the dust ruffle caught my eye. Feeling the pump knots on various locations of my head—total to that point on pump knots: three—I couldn't help but be bemused for a second at all the vomit. As I lifted the contaminated dust ruffle I almost shit my pants: there was the fucking lockbox! Just as my cousin Jessica had described it. I started to almost hyperventilate from excitement.

Finally, we could get the fuck out of there! I knew I didn't have the key, but I would worry about that later, citing crowbars in my mind as an eventual possibility. I wrapped the lockbox up in the big comfy blanket I had brought with me from home. Then I walked right out of the bedroom past my aunt and the boys with what looked like an armful of blanket. As I scurried for the front door mumbling that I needed something to drink with electrolytes in it, Jacob offered to drive me considering my beat-up and hungover condition. My aunt yelled out for us to pick her up a pack of cigarettes. My son stayed at the apartment with her. She is so clueless, I thought. *All she ever thinks about is herself!* We went first to a store to get the drink and the cigarettes, then to a remote pull off to see about getting that lockbox open. For the sake of seeming more realistic, I wish I could tell you that we had a hell of a time getting that sucker open, but we did not. In fact, as soon as I plopped it down in the back hatch of the van it flew the fuck open! My heart was pounding. Would we find the remaining $5,100?

Unfortunately, we didn't, but then we had been warned that it might not all be there, given my aunt's propensity for writing out money orders to herself. There was however $3,100 still there amongst all sorts of papers and the like. Removing the remaining money, we drove back to my aunt's. Jacob handed her the requested cigarettes and I put the lockbox back where I had found it. Giving my son the nod that it was over, he started getting up and about as I was packing personal belongings back into the Batman bag. My aunt asked in a worried tone if we were leaving. "Oh no," I exclaimed, "but I sure could go for a biscuit to settle my alcohol-ravaged stomach. Why don't we go get some breakfast?" I asked the boys. "Sure," they both said, in support of me. Of course, only thinking of herself once again my aunt said, "Get me a strawberry milkshake." Wow, my aunt, true to her lifelong pattern, never asked, just demanded. She didn't request. She expected. She never gave, only took.

Once inside the van, the boys and I did in fact go get breakfast, part of which was a strawberry milkshake, but only because my son thought that sounded pretty good. Then I took over driving and I drove straight home to Tennessee. I have to wonder, considering it's a two-and-a-half-hour drive, how long my aunt sat in her recliner that morning, puffing her free cigarettes, waiting on that free milkshake before it hit her that something was terribly wrong.

We were almost all the way back home to Tennessee when my boyfriend called my cell phone and told me my aunt had just called him and told him I "robbed" her of $5,100 and that now my daddy wouldn't have a headstone. Even now, she continued to lie. It didn't surprise me, but damn. She was going to tack the $2,000 she had already spent onto the sum she told people I "robbed" her of. I can tell you, with two people as my witness, that there was only ever $3,100, of which I didn't keep one cent. Furthermore, I kept not one gun, not one bullet for myself. Not only did I not keep any of it, I never crossed state lines with any of it.

After all, it wasn't mine, it wasn't my dad's and it damn sure wasn't my aunt's! I promise I'm not just being an elusive asshole on purpose about what I did do with it, it's just that is someone else's story now and not mine to tell.

All in all, I have to say, it was a caper that even Joel Hubbard would have been proud of.

EPILOGUE

THERE IS AN OLD CLICHÉ that love is stronger than hate, but that's a precarious proclamation. Love is preferable to hate, in that it feels much better and doesn't make us sick inside the way hate does. I think when love fails it's because whether we realize it or not we often have expectations and preconceived notions about what love is supposed to be. There are several definitions for the word if you just look it up online, but really love in its original, pure and raw state is an unselfish, loyal and benevolent concern for another. How often are any of us willing to give on that level without expecting something in return? I believe God is Love and that we're the ones with all the convoluted preferences and ideas about it. We form dying allegiances to the concepts we have about love, more often than we practice or participate in the real thing.

Personally, I'm rooting for all of us to make it. I try not to approach life with an attitude of being in competition with anybody, as if there were an "us" and "them." There is only an all. We all are born. We all suffer. We all seek happiness while we're here.

We all die. The truth of it *all*, ends there. While I'm here though, I will no longer tolerate chaos, drama, negativity or abuse in my life from anybody. I deserve more than that. We *all* do. I know I have certain types of people reading this book who would agree. Do you know who they are? They're survivors! Survivors of many things. Recovering alcoholics. Recovering drug addicts. People recovering from the psychological effects of abuse, rape and incest. People who have overcome extreme poverty and degraded social status.

Survivors are usually recovering from something and so the two words intermingle. The reason is as clear as a bell to me, though. Survival is a state of mind. The actual process of survival is a byproduct of that state of mind, that separates the survivors from the "woe is me" motherfuckers who often get caught in the trap of self-perpetuating their troubles. Survivors are always recovering; it's why we're called survivors. We are recovering from something; if we weren't there wouldn't have been anything to have to survive in the first place.

It is okay to let go of toxic people, even family—especially family! You do not owe allegiance to blood relations when they are hurting or abusing you. There is an old saying that you can't choose your family, but I say to hell with that! We choose everything. We choose to be happy or not. We choose to be positive or not. We choose to live healthy lifestyles or not. So yes, we can choose our family and some of us most certainly should. We are always free to choose, just not free from the consequences of those choices. So, choose wisely. The only thing irreplaceable in this equation is your life. Every circumstance, obstacle, mistake, or person who brought you to this pain can be replaced by your choice to seek better things for yourself. Choose recovery, health (both emotional and physical), happiness and love. We all have our demons to battle. Even in the midst of the battle though, God's gifts are unimaginable once we are open to receiving them.

A lot of times we think we are open, but we aren't. We put conditions on things and try to make bargains with God, but that is not the same as being open. Open is when God tells you something, or shows you something that He intends for you and it seems impossible to you at the time, but you go ahead and believe in it enough to act on it anyway. Pushing forward and on until it materializes. After the pain and past the numb, there is the possibility of pleasure and peace. We can create that for ourselves, by working on ourselves. We are not powerless. We cannot change other people, that is up to them, but we can walk away when and if we need to. Happiness is not outside ourselves; it lies within, sometimes buried. We must cultivate it, believe in it, imitate it, until it is just our state of mind. Happiness doesn't mean perfect, though. It's more of a positive state of awareness that doesn't need "perfect" to be happy. If you know yourself with complete, honest, humble self-awareness you can get as close as is humanly possible to the Truth, and that trumps perfect any day.

Everyone deserves an authentic experience from within, for without that there isn't proof of anything. Find your way in this world. It is worth the effort, and it is your way to find after all. It works. How else could I have once been the daughter of a white-sheeted ghoul, but now I am the mother of a beautiful, sixty-something-pound lump of brown sugar?

What doesn't kill you transforms you. What it transforms you into, is up to you.

CPSIA information can be obtained
at www.ICGtesting.com
Printed in the USA
LVHW090229240620
658845LV00001B/117